Contours of Christian Philosophy
C. STEPHEN EVANS, *Series Editor*

EPISTEMOLOGY: The Justification of Belief *David L. Wolfe*
METAPHYSICS: Constructing a World View *William Hasker*
ETHICS: Approaching Moral Decisions *Arthur F. Holmes*
PHILOSOPHY OF RELIGION: Thinking about Faith
C. Stephen Evans
PHILOSOPHY OF SCIENCE: The Natural Sciences in
Christian Perspective *Del Ratzsch*
PHILOSOPHY OF EDUCATION: Issues and Options
Michael L. Peterson

Contours of Christian Philosophy
C. STEPHEN EVANS, *Series Editor*

Philosophy
of
Education

Issues
and Options

Michael L. Peterson

InterVarsity Press
Downers Grove, Illinois, U.S.A.
Leicester, England

InterVarsity Press
P.O. Box 1400, Downers Grove, Illinois 60515, U.S.A.
38 De Montfort Street, Leicester LE1 7GP, England

InterVarsity Press, U.S.A., is the book-publishing division of Inter-Varsity Christian Fellowship, a student movement active on campus at hundreds of universities, colleges and schools of nursing. For information about local and regional activities, write IVCF, 6400 Schroeder Road, Madison, WI 53707-7895.

Inter-Varsity Press, England, is the publishing division of the Universities and Colleges Christian Fellowship (formerly the Inter-Varsity Fellowship), a student movement linking Christian Unions in universities and colleges throughout the British Isles, and a member movement of the International Fellowship of Evangelical Students. For information about local and national activities in Great Britain write to UCCF, 38 De Montfort Street, Leicester LE1 7GP.

Distributed in Canada through InterVarsity Press, 860 Denison St., Unit 3, Markham, Ontario L3R 4H1, Canada.

ISBNs: USA 0-87784-345-7   USA 0-87784-339-2 (Contours of Christian Philosophy set)
       UK 0-85110-766-4

Printed in the United States of America

British Library Cataloguing in Publication Data

Peterson, Michael L.
    Philosophy of education: issues and
    options.—(Contours of Christian
    philosophy)
    1. Church and education
    I. Title II. Series
    261   LC368

    ISBN 0-85110-766-4

Library of Congress Cataloging in Publication Data

Peterson, Michael L., 1950-
    Philosophy of education.

    (Contours of Christian philosophy)
    Bibliography: p.
    1. Education (Christian theology).   2. Education—
Philosophy.   I. Title.   II. Series.
BT738.17.P48   1986   370'.1   86-21011
ISBN 0-87784-345-7

18	17	16	15	14	13	12	11	10	9	8	7	6	5	4	3	2	1
99	98	97	96	95	94	93	92	91	90	89	88	87	86				

*To the faculty
of Asbury College*

GENERAL PREFACE

The Contours of Christian Philosophy series will consist of short introductory-level textbooks in the various fields of philosophy. These books will introduce readers to major problems and alternative ways of dealing with those problems. These books, however, will differ from most in that they will evaluate alternative viewpoints not only with regard to their general strength, but also with regard to their value in the construction of a Christian world and life view. Thus, the books will explore the implications of the various views for Christian theology as well as the implications that Christian convictions might have for the philosophical issues discussed. It is crucial that Christians attain a greater degree of philosophical awareness in order to improve the quality of general scholarship and evangelical theology. My hope is that this series will contribute to that end.

Although the books are intended as examples of Christian scholarship, it is hoped that they will be of value to others as well; these issues should concern all thoughtful persons. The assumption which underlies this hope is that complete neutrality in philosophy is neither possible nor desirable. Philosophical work always reflects a person's deepest commitments. Such commitments, however, do not preclude a genuine striving for critical honesty.

C. Stephen Evans
Series Editor

1. What Is Philosophy of Education? *13*
   Why Study Theory? *14*
   Philosophy and Educational Theory *17*
   Preliminary Definitions and Distinctions *18*

2. Traditional Philosophies of Education *23*
   Idealism: Minds and Ideas *25*
   Idealism and the Educative Process *27*
   Evaluating Idealism *29*
   Naturalism: Objects and Order *31*
   Naturalism and the Educative Process *33*
   Evaluating Naturalism *38*
   Neo-Thomism: Being and Essence *41*
   Neo-Thomism and the Educative Process *45*
   Evaluating Neo-Thomism *47*

3. Contemporary Philosophies of Education *51*
   Experimentalism: Experience and Society *52*
   Experimentalism and the Educative Process *55*
   Evaluating Experimentalism *59*
   Existentialism: Individual and Choice *63*
   Existentialism and the Educative Process *66*
   Evaluating Existentialism *69*
   Philosophical Analysis: Logic and Linguistics *71*
   Philosophical Analysis and the Educative Process *73*
   Evaluating Philosophical Analysis *76*

4. Toward a Christian Perspective on Education *79*
   Christianity and Metaphysics *80*
   Christianity and Epistemology *83*
   Christianity and Axiology *84*
   A Christian Justification of Education *87*

Christianity and the Curriculum   88
Christianity, Teaching and Learning   91
Christianity and Value Education   94

5. Issues in Educational Theory   97
Liberal Learning and General Education   98
The Integration of Faith and Learning   102
Education in Morals and Values   107
Pedagogy and the Educational Enterprise   113

6. Issues in Educational Practice   117
Liberal Education and Vocational Training   118
Public and Private Education   120
Academic Rights and Freedoms   124
Teaching and Indoctrination   128

7. Christianity and the Pursuit of Excellence   131
Education as Product and Process   132
Intellect in the Service of Christ   138

Notes   141

Further Reading   151

AUTHOR'S PREFACE

Although I did not know it then, this book began when I was an undergraduate at Asbury College. By both precept and example, the faculty enabled me to glimpse the larger meaning of education within a Christian world view. Among those who contributed to my early thinking, President Dennis Kinlaw, Professor James Hamilton and Professor Paul Denlinger were especially influential.

Others have also been important to the development of the book. Since my college days, I have profited from many long talks about education with Paul Vincent and Edward Madden. Traces of their thought can be found throughout the following pages. During the early stages of writing, the comments of Ralph Joly and Timothy Thomas were very helpful. Stephen Evans, Arthur Holmes and David Wolfe commented on the entire first draft, making the final product much better than it would have been. Cheryl Smith carefully keyed the manuscript into a computer so that I could make revisions more easily. I am grateful to the Faculty Research and Development Committee of Asbury College for granting a work leave during the fall of 1984 so that I could complete the book.

My family also had a hand in the book. My wife, Rebecca, patiently endured its preparation; and my young sons, Aaron and Adam, not so patiently.

Indebted to all who were in any way connected to this work, I still must dedicate it to that group of special people among whom it was born—the faculty of Asbury College.

1

What Is Philosophy of Education?

*O*n one occasion Aristotle was asked how much educated people were superior to those uneducated: "As much," he replied, "as the living are to the dead."[1] The words of the great teacher remind us that there is hardly a more powerful force than education. In a real sense, education provides the mind with life and shapes the whole person.

Most people in the West spend at least eleven years of their lives in formal education. Many extend their education through college or beyond. It is necessary, therefore, to think carefully about the role of education. In the words of Abraham Lincoln, the discussion of education is "the most important subject which we, as a people, can be engaged in."[2]

All sorts of questions immediately arise: What form should education take? Can values be taught? What is the knowledge most worth having? Is it possible to integrate learning with faith? These and other important questions quickly move us from the practical level to the theoretical. The theory of education is a matter about which responsible people disagree. Although there is no consensus about the nature and purpose of education, there is hope that thoughtful persons can gain some insight through reasonable dialog.

Why Study Theory?
As a culture, we are not very reflective. We are more concerned with actions and results than with theory, with "how" rather than "why." This prejudice has been detrimental to the educational enterprise. Charles Silberman claims that our educational milieu suffers from "mindlessness," charging that it uncritically prizes technique over understanding and progress over goals.[3] Modern educators have been so busy developing new instruments for measuring intelligence and aptitude, exploring creative methods for teaching mathematics to elementary schoolchildren and seeking more efficient ways to complete a college degree that they have seldom stopped to ask why such things are desirable.

Few have addressed the larger meaning of education. Lawrence Cremin points this out, writing of the United States but making a statement which is widely true in the West:

Too few educational leaders in the United States are genuinely preoccupied with educational issues because they have no clear ideas about education. And if we look at the way these leaders have been recruited and trained, there is little that would lead us to expect otherwise. They have too often been managers, facilitators, politicians in the narrowest sense. They have been concerned with building buildings, balancing budgets, and pacifying parents, but they have not been prepared to spark a great public dialogue about the ends and means of education. And in the absence of such dialogue, large segments of the public have had, at best, a limited understanding of the ways and wherefores of popular schooling.[4]

Although there is occasional talk of nurturing our educators in the literature of education, more attention is needed. The following questions must be raised: What is the purpose of education? What goals do new techniques and methods serve? What kind of person is our educational system supposed to produce? These are theoretical questions which force us to articulate and expand our basic commitments. If our schools are to be productive, we must recover the relationship between educational theory and practice.

Theory gives direction to practice. To paraphrase Kant, practice without theory is blind. Without theory, responses to problems will be arbitrary and short-sighted. A coherent theory is required to guide our thinking about education. Theory guides by establishing the aims of education and projecting basic ways in which these ends can be reached. Concrete decisions—such as whether sex education should be conducted in middle schools or whether a college should add a certain program of instruction—can be made according to a theoretical framework.

In the final analysis, no educational practices can proceed without theory. Every policy and procedure, whether we realize it or not, is laden with some conception of what education is all about and how it should perform its task. When these concepts are brought to light, we can more intelligently assess our educational activities. The correct route, then, is for us to maintain the intimate relationship between theory and practice, and to consider the options among theories of education. Nothing could be more practical.

Practice has a reciprocal impact on theory. Practice can "test" a theory; it can validate or invalidate educational concepts and proposals. A fine-sounding theory may run into difficulties in practice and thus cause us to rethink, modify or perhaps even relinquish our original ideas. Every educational theory has to encounter the hard realities of ordinary life and stand or fall according to its adequacy to human experience. To extend our paraphrase of Kant, theory without practice is empty.

Actually, exploring the general ideas which give direction to specific educational policies and practices does not go far enough. For example, take the policy of nondiscrimination in hiring teachers and educating students. This policy can be deduced from the concepts of the dignity of all human beings and of fair treatment. But how did we obtain these concepts? They must still be defined by a more comprehensive philosophy of life. But there are competing views of life which vie for our allegiance. Thus, the particular world and life view which one adopts determines how the concepts of human dignity and fairness are defined. Not only are educational policy and practice subordinate to educational theory, but educational theory itself is born out of a larger world view. We can schematize these relationships as follows:

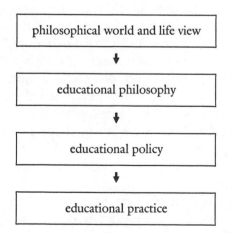

A general educational theory does not always dictate specific decisions but provides a way of thinking about policies and practices. Certainly no decisions can have clear direction without reference to some educational theory. And no educational theory can have a firm foundation apart from some fundamental philosophical perspective.

Philosophy and Educational Theory

Philosophy is primarily concerned with theory, the examination of ideas and ideals. Ideas about the meaning of the human venture, the existence of God, the nature of knowledge, the principles of morality, the most desirable social structure—all of these and more fit together into a comprehensive point of view. Interestingly, respectable thinkers differ widely on such subjects. And the philosophical position one holds significantly influences one's thoughts on education. Indeed, the very nature of the "educational enterprise" is typically redefined by each philosophical perspective.

Therefore, a full-scale study of educational theory ushers us to the threshold of philosophy. *The philosophy of education is the attempt to bring the insights and methods of philosophy to bear on the educational enterprise.* This pursuit rests on the confidence that serious persons can, by taking thought, shape their educational institutions and, through them, their destiny.

Professional educators, both present and future, must be able to think intelligently about the large questions which underlie educational methods and goals. Teachers, counselors, administrators and curriculum specialists should be familiar with the issues regarding the nature of reality and the purpose of life. When students of educational philosophy have found their way through these basic issues, then they are in a position to select intelligently the aims of education and choose effectively the pedagogical methods which promote them.

Noneducators can also benefit from the philosophy of education. While educators certainly need a conceptual framework to guide their activities, every thoughtful individual needs a coherent view of life and the world. Philosophy of education may offer the first opportunity to ponder life's great questions or aid in the formulation of educational and career goals. It may even provide greater motivation for study and achievement. Philosophy of education, then, allows professionals and nonprofessionals to become familiar with the major philosophies of life and invites them to think through a host of educational issues.

From a Christian perspective, the philosophy of education is extremely important. Contemporary Christians rightly feel obliged to respond to a multitude of current educational issues, such as the creation-evolution debate in American schools or the apparent lack of sound moral training in public education. Many Christians wrestle with the decision of whether to attend, or to encourage their children to attend, a Christian or other private school rather than a state school. Yet they need more than a convenient set of answers to immediate problems. They need a whole way of thinking about education—a philosophy which relates their religious commitment to educational concerns.

The main point of contact between educational philosophy and Christianity is that they both address the same basic questions: the meaning of life, the nature of morality, the worth of knowledge and so on. There is a variety of answers to these questions. Each group of answers forms a distinct point of view, which, in turn, generates implications for education.

This book presents the major positions in the philosophy of education and examines their relationship to the Christian faith. On some matters it may turn out that the conscientious Christian can take only one position; on other issues there may be a range of acceptable positions. The purpose of this study, then, is not to dictate opinions, but to open up a way of thinking about the relevant subjects.

Preliminary Definitions and Distinctions

Philosophy is both a subject matter and an activity. In other words, it is a field of inquiry with a distinctive content and a certain method. These two dimensions of philosophy have an impact on educational theory at key points.

As a *subject matter,* philosophy contains the great ongoing dialog on life's most important questions. Part of the significance of philosophy is that it holds before us basic problems and concerns which, when conscientiously explored, bring enlightenment and sensitivity. Clusters of related questions together with their major answers form the main branches of philosophy: metaphysics, epistemology and axiology.

The branch of philosophy known as metaphysics examines such questions as "What exists?" and "What is the nature of reality?" Broadly conceived, metaphysics inquires into such far-reaching subjects as the existence of God and the meaning of being human.[5] Metaphysics is central to the educational enterprise because education is ultimately designed according to what a society or group considers reality to be. Different perspectives on the structure of reality lead to divergent approaches to education. Consider the distinct educational orientations which emerge from the view that a person is a rational and spiritual being, on the one hand, and from the view that a person is merely a complex animal, on the other.

Epistemology is the branch of philosophy which deals with questions of knowledge: What is truth? What are the sources of knowledge? How do we know? Concerns of this sort probe into the nature and validity of human knowledge.[6] Obviously, epistemological issues are critical to educational theory. Since education deals in knowledge, the epistemological assumptions held by an educator and educational system will shape pedagogical aims and methodologies. For example, the assumption that sensory experience is the only source of knowledge encourages teaching methods which stress practical, hands-on experience for the students. But the assumption that insight and intuition also provide knowledge tends to generate teaching methods which incorporate critical thinking and exposure to abstract ideas.

The question "What is valuable?" characterizes the area of philosophy known as axiology. We are undeniably valuing beings, preferring some things over others. Ethics is the area of axiology which studies what is morally good or preferable in both character and conduct.[7] Aesthetics treats questions related to the concept of the beautiful. Aesthetics explores what it means to create and appreciate beauty in various artistic contexts. There is an intimate connection between axiology and education. After all, much education revolves around the formation of preferences which extend into the spheres of morality and taste. The axiological position taken by an educator or educational community influences classroom content and procedure, and can affect the entire curriculum structure. For example, great differences exist between educators who take morality to be universal and essentially linked to religion and those who take morality to be relative to individuals and cultures. The former tend to require that the student learn a particular religious viewpoint as a basis for a certain moral standard. The latter typically strive for utter neutrality in discussing ethical issues.

Philosophy as an *activity* or method involves several kinds of intellectual functions: the synthetic, the analytic, the descriptive and the normative. Philosophers differ over the way these activities are related and their comparative importance. Some identify the proper way of doing philosophy with one specific type of thinking activity; others would propose a combination of types. Without settling any of these issues here, let us survey the activities in question.

The synthetic dimension of philosophical thinking seeks a comprehensive view of things. It attempts to weave together all of our knowledge and insight about the world into a systematic, unified perspective. Synoptic thinking sees life and the universe as a whole rather than as fragmented; it expresses the desire to formulate a world view.[8] A world view contains interrelated assumptions about the nature of reality, knowledge and value, and can be further expanded into concepts of society, science, art and so forth. In philosophy of education, the synthetic function assembles a total picture of human existence and of how learning is to be conducted.

Analytic thinking in philosophy seeks to understand the assumptions and methods upon which common sense and science depend. It even turns attention inward to the basic elements of philosophy itself, attempting to gain a clear conception of the meaning of terms and to develop a careful examination of arguments. Without a grasp of the meaning of such terms as *true, real, mind, matter, good* and *evil,* philosophical dialog can be ambiguous or vague. And without a rigorous understanding of the principles of valid argument, the case for some position could be incoherent or misleading. The analytic dimension of philosophy of education raises questions about the meaning of such crucial terms as *learning, schooling, training* and *indoctrination.* It scrutinizes the main arguments for competing philosophical positions as well as for rival educational theories.

Descriptive activity in philosophy attempts to represent accurately "what is the case." After all, some of the most significant facts about ourselves as human beings are not discoverable by scientific procedures. Many of these facts, which are not immediately obvious, must be carefully exposed and properly described. As Robert Beck says, "Facts must be revealed, the implicit made explicit, and the misinterpreted or uninterpreted brought forward for examination."[9] Description in philosophy produces accounts, say, of how conscience operates or of how perception occurs. In philosophy of education this descriptive activity is interested, for example, in articulating the structure of human knowledge and tracing the developmental stages of the child to determine at which stage certain kinds of subjects can be taught.

The normative function of philosophical thinking is perhaps closest to the original spirit of philosophy. It seeks to provide standards and ideals as guides for our individual and collective lives. Within the context of education, the prescriptive function enables us to contemplate the ethical and aesthetic values which should be transmitted to students and which should guide the conduct of teachers and administrators. Fundamentally, of course, the normative function in philosophy of education tries to envision what kind of persons education is trying to develop and what kind of society we ought to have.

The project of this book is to lead the reader progressively into the philosophy of education, showing throughout the relevance of a Christian point of view. However, it does not present either philosophy or Christianity merely as bodies of belief to be learned; rather, it invites the reader to engage in the actual process of thinking through philosophical issues from a Christian perspective. A Christian philosophy of education, like philosophy at large, is not just a subject matter but an activity. Hence the book is truly an introduction, presenting preliminary material and then inviting the reader to consider many issues which lie beyond its scope.

2

Traditional Philosophies of Education

*I*n spite of much agreement on the basic questions of philosophy, diversity prevails regarding the answers to those questions. Questions regarding the nature of reality, knowledge and value are answered in distinctive ways by different schools of thought, since they all come at the questions from different frames of reference.

Each philosophical perspective is formed by certain metaphysical, epistemological and axiological assumptions. These assumptions, in turn, have implications for a host of important subjects, such as politics, science and education. This is how a fundamental philosophy provides a comprehensive view of the world.

Disagreements about the nature of reality, knowledge and value lead to significant disagreement on educational matters. The metaphysical position of a given philosophy, by virtue of projecting a picture of reality, supplies a conception of the nature of humanity and of what there is to be known. Thus every philosophy indicates something about the "ends" or aims of human education and the subject matter. The epistemological preference of a given philosophy favors certain styles of learning and methods of teaching. It specifies how the acquisition of knowledge should take place. The axiological commitments of a philosophical perspective provide an understanding of what kind of character should be developed and what kinds of taste should be cultivated. A full-blown philosophy of education, then, is a unified set of philosophical assumptions together with their implications for the educational enterprise.[1]

This chapter and the next will consider six prominent philosophies which have implications for education: idealism, naturalism, Neo-Thomism, experimentalism, existentialism and philosophical analysis. The former three are traditional in the sense that they offer global interpretations of all existence. The latter three are modern in that they deny that a comprehensive world view is possible, but nonetheless make a number of presumptions about the nature of reality, knowledge and value. To be sure, other philosophical positions (for example, Hinduism) have educational implications. However, these viewpoints have not been very influential in Western educational systems and thus lie beyond the scope of this book.

These two chapters will use a threefold format for discussing each view. First, each philosophical perspective is presented with emphasis given to its metaphysical, epistemological and axiological assumptions. Second, the educational implications of each perspective are explored, particularly those regarding educational aims and curricula, styles of teaching and learning, and methods of ethical and aesthetic training. Third, each perspective is briefly evaluated according to its philosophical adequacy, educational appropriateness and theological correctness.[2] For each philosophical view, one or two representative thinkers are used as the basis of discussion.

Idealism: Minds and Ideas

An idealist believes that reality is composed of minds, ideas or selves rather than material things. As William Hocking has said, the term "idea-ism" would be more to the point than "idealism."[3] The central metaphysical affirmation of idealism is that physical objects are either unreal in themselves or much less real than ideas. While idealism may seem strange at first, it has been held in one form or another by some great thinkers, past and present, East and West. George Berkeley, G. W. F. Hegel and S. Radhakrishnan all held idealistic positions.

One corollary of idealism is that the essence of humanity is spiritual or mental. It is human nature to think, feel and value. Immanuel Kant is a major representative of this view, one who made important contributions to educational philosophy. His theory that personhood has intrinsic worth is a lofty and pure expression of idealistic thinking. For Kant, neither the body nor physical attributes are relevant to the ultimate value of a human being; it is the soul or mind which truly constitutes one's nature.

Most idealistic philosophers hold that the universe is a rational system, or at least that we must think of it in these terms. Kant makes this an epistemological thesis, holding that human reason is the organizing and unifying factor in all knowledge. Reason renders the world intelligible by imposing categories on our experience. When our senses represent the world to us, the mind interprets them through the forms of space and time, and the categories of quantity, quality and so on. Such concepts are innate in the structure of our consciousness and thus create the structure of knowledge.

For idealists, epistemology is primarily a theory about how the finite human mind acquires truth or how it comes into contact with God's mind. Historically, idealism has been concerned to deny skepticism and assure the possibility of success in the knowledge venture. Most idealists, including Kant, have even asserted that there are universal truths.

In addition to stressing the role of the mind as the organizer of thoughts, some idealists also emphasize the emerging quality of selfhood which each human being should experience. Finite selves are either said to be miniature replicas of God conceived as the Absolute Self or encouraged to emulate some transcendent model of personhood. These versions of idealism accent the moral, aesthetic and emotional aspects of our being as well as the purely intellectual.

The axiology, or theory of value, which idealists hold fits naturally with their views of reality and knowledge. For idealists, ethical and aesthetic values are absolute and unchanging. Although many idealists say that the source of these values is the Infinite Person, or God, Kant says that they originate in the structure of rationality itself. A perfect standard of goodness is therefore available to us. In fact, Kant posits belief in the existence of God on the basis of his moral theory. Critical of the traditional proofs of God's existence, he holds that rational and moral beings simply must think of God as making the moral life meaningful.

The general outline of idealistic ethics and aesthetics is not difficult to plot. Kant holds that all truly moral choices must not be made on the basis of egocentric interests but must reflect what is universally right for all humankind.[4] For Kant, as for most idealists, aesthetics is the companion to ethics: the worth of a work of art lies in how well it expresses an ideal. Kant claims that the secret to artistic creation and aesthetic taste is the ability to bring a particular under a general norm or rule, what he calls judgment.

Whether in painting, sculpture, music, poetry or other art forms, idealistic artists generally think of themselves as "idealizing" something, of using a singular instance to embody a larger ideal. Idealistic artists might even minimize blemishes or remove idiosyncratic traits from the object they are creating so that it better expresses the ideal. Of course, the ideal is never fully realizable in experience. Thus the realm of art is not merely the sensory world but the world of intellect in which genius or talent applies rules of practice to the work at hand.[5]

Idealism and the Educative Process

Idealism holds that the world is rational and purposeful; indeed for many idealists the world is deeply personal. The aim of education, then, is the full intellectual, moral and spiritual development of the student. To the extent that students emulate the Divine Being or realize ideals of personhood they will have developed correctly. According to Kant, students should acquire discipline and self-mastery, possess mental skills and have a firm character and good will. These dispositions are to serve the proper ends of humankind. Clearly students need practical skills to navigate in the everyday world, but the main orientation is toward the ideal, perfect, transcendent realm which truly defines human existence.[6]

For Kant, as for most idealists, the curriculum should be strongly intellectual. It should enable students to be adept with ideas and symbols, and should acquaint them with positive models (exemplars, heroes and heroines) so that their personhood grows and flourishes. The favored courses for eliciting qualities of personhood and reflecting the rational structure of the cosmos include literature, art, intellectual history, philosophy, religion and even mathematics. At the college level such studies are called the humanities. But Kant's recommendations can be met at elementary and secondary levels as long as instruction stimulates mental skills and cultivates sound personhood.[7]

Typical idealists tend to prefer teaching methods which are based on pure intellectual activity rather than on practical or concrete experience. Lectures and discussions are recommended as the primary classroom activities. Reading and research in the library are extremely important. Field trips, "hands-on" experiences, classroom demonstrations and the like are de-emphasized.

Of course, as Kant indicates, aesthetic skills necessitate less instruction and more example and practice. While detractors of idealism say it creates an "ivory tower" situation for teachers and learners, Kant and others insist that the mission of education is to impart mental skills which the students will use to cope with everyday life. Furthermore, idealists defend themselves by saying that the emphasis on the ideal realm of truth, goodness and beauty helps students to live a whole and enriched life.[8]

The teacher, for idealism, does more than simply initiate the pupils into abstract or intuitive thinking. He or she is strategically placed in front of the pupils as a model self who is to help them attain fuller selfhood. Kant particularly advocates modeling freedom, autonomy and pure motives. Teachers and administrators, moreover, have a responsibility to create a healthy "psychological environment" among students; their personhood is nourished in a climate of rapport and mutual respect.

The value theory of idealism advocates specific ways to shape moral character and refine aesthetic taste. In moral education, universal ethical principles are communicated to the student—both through didactic instruction and exemplary action—so that they might be applied in concrete situations. Useful pedagogical tools include examples and lessons found in fairy tales, fiction and biography. Although some idealists believe social wisdom (traditions, cultural conventions and so forth) is the repository of moral principles, Kant was suspicious of this. He feared rivalry and competitiveness between existing peoples and nations. Thus, he idealized the "unity of selves" or moral community as transcending personal and national interests.

The idealist conceives of art as the idealization of the world and measures its value in terms of its success in capturing the universal amidst the particulars of everyday life. For Kant, neither aesthetic taste nor creative talent can be directly communicated. Key pedagogical approaches are exposing the student to great art, explaining how it conforms to certain universal rules and letting the student practice creating beautiful art. Artistic sensibility is a unity of intellectual and affective elements.

Evaluating Idealism

The endorsement of idealistic philosophy by many thinkers in the Orient and the Occident must be taken seriously. They believe that idealism is an adequate account of the rationality and meaningfulness of the world, and of the dignity and worth of the human self. They see it as providing a basis for moral and religious values by making them structural features of the universe. Some think it explains the existence of a Being beyond ourselves.

Idealists, however, have not fully established their fundamental claim that reality is somehow dependent on mind. Berkeleyan idealists hold that objects are dependent on consciousness for their very existence. Kantian idealists hold that objects are dependent on mind for their rational structure. Now it is one thing to claim that reality is rationally understandable and a much stronger claim to say, as Berkeley and Kant do in their own ways, that reality is essentially mental. We ordinarily make a distinction between thought about our environment and the external environment itself, the perceiver and the perceived.[9] So it is difficult to see how idealists can establish either that what makes a thing real is its presence in consciousness or that what gives a thing its intelligibility is the mind's attribution of categories.

Surely there is a presumption in favor of some of humankind's most basic beliefs which idealism contradicts. Many of these beliefs are about the material world: that there are physical objects independent of our minds and that they have an inherent structure which registers in human thought. It is hard to imagine what argument could possibly overturn these convictions. By making all reality dependent on mind in one way or another, idealism devalues the external dimension of reality in which we find ourselves. Thus idealism drives its epistemology to an ontological dead end.

It is not surprising that idealistic educational theory relies heavily on abstract and "bookish" methods, since its basic assumption is that reality is somehow dependent on mind. Kant believes that education is basically "formal training."[10] Yet this is an imbalanced perspective on the relation of mental and material factors and does not adequately take into account the practical and experiential aspect of our humanity.

Another concern is that idealistic educational philosophy tends to sustain the status quo. The assumption that there is a higher, changeless Reality above the vacillating world inclines many idealists to view the social function of the school to be preserving the heritage of the past. The school is not typically seen as an agent of social change or reconstruction. Kant, however, is not a preservationist. His vision of the human race includes revising current realities according to an ideal.

The relation of idealism to Christianity is intriguing. While idealism appears to accommodate many Christian beliefs, it distorts them in peculiar ways. For instance, the idealists affirmation of a Supreme Being fits, on the face of it, with the historic Christian doctrine of God. Yet many theologians say that a concept of God as the Supreme Mind is an intellectualized one which excludes concepts of grace and redeeming love.

Kant views Christianity as one manifestation of true religion, which "is everywhere the same." True religion for Kant is simply morality conceived as the will of God. Morality does not presuppose the validity of religious belief, but vice versa.[11] Kant held that the proper motive for being moral is not the fear or love of God, but a sense of duty. Yet this makes the rest of theology peripheral to morality.

Kant's stern view of God carries over into his theory of how religion should be introduced to children. He believes that young children are not capable of understanding many religious ideas because such ideas rest on a knowledge of moral duty and an understanding of the abstractions of theology. He recommends, therefore, that we should instruct the young about the ends of humanity and convey only a minimal idea of the Supreme Being.

Another problem is that most versions of idealism seem unable to generate a proper view of religious faith. In fact, some idealists (Brand Blanchard, for example) adopt a rationalism which is hostile to any faith that cannot be proved with logical certainty. Kant's critical idealism attempts to bring "religion within the bounds of reason alone." Ironically, Kant wanted a totally rational religion but denied that the truths of natural theology can be rationally proved. The strength of such idealistic views is their insistence that religious beliefs be reasonable. However, they lack an adequate analysis of the relation of faith and reason.

A final Christian criticism of idealism relates to its view of matter. Idealists typically deny that physical objects exist or that we can have valid knowledge of their natures. Historic Christianity, to the contrary, affirms both the reality of physical things and our God-given ability to understand them. Kantianism admits that there are objects "out there" but does not believe that we can know what they are in themselves. So although Kant's idealism accents many important epistemological points, it ultimately fails to do justice to the material aspect of the created order.

Naturalism: Objects and Order
Naturalism can be seen as the polar opposite of idealism. It holds that nature alone is real, that all reality is physical or material. The converse of this claim is that there are no nonmaterial things: there is no realm of immaterial spirit or mind; there is no God or supreme being. Every tenet of naturalistic metaphysics follows from the belief that matter is the sole reality and is eternal: the cosmos is an ordered system of cause and effect; a

human being is a complex physical organism; death means personal extinction.

Advocates of naturalism span the centuries, from Lucretius through Thomas Hobbes and David Hume to Charles Darwin and Karl Marx. In the present day, naturalism is probably the dominant philosophical perspective, endorsed by such thinkers as R. B. Perry and J. J. C. Smart. Although these thinkers differ in emphasis and detail, they share the common naturalistic or materialistic insight. A popular contemporary proponent for naturalism is Carl Sagan.

Ernest Nagel represents naturalism when he affirms "the existential and causal primacy of organized matter."[12] All qualities and events are dependent on the configurations of matter. Humanity is, for Nagel, a relatively temporary phenomenon in our part of the cosmos. Explaining that the physical and physiological conditions for human existence have not and will not always endure, he admits that "human destiny is an episode between two oblivions."[13]

Nagel's theory of knowledge is empiricism: the view that knowledge comes exclusively through the senses. Like almost all modern empiricists, Nagel takes science as the theory's chief manifestation, since observation, experiment and public verifiability extend the fundamental reliance on the senses. The goal of the empirical method is to discover the regularities of the natural world and codify them into lawlike generalizations.

Nagel denies that values reflect any ultimate or universal truths. Moral standards are methods of adjudicating human conflicts. Hence moral norms are tools for the intelligent management of the various interests and energies of human nature. The subjective needs which individuals feel are, in turn, amenable to conditioning by society. This position foreshadows the theory of emotivism which asserts that moral and aesthetic claims express the subjective states of persons and are not derived, say, from a supernatural realm.

Most naturalists acknowledge certain moral traits which most cultures tend to cultivate: loyalty, honesty, discipline and so forth. Aesthetic ideals originate in a similar way. For Nagel, the fact that many cultures seem to hold the same basic values, differing only in particular prescriptions, is explained by the fact that human nature is basically the same everywhere. Human nature, in turn, is simply a facet of the overall natural world. Hence nature is the sole ground of value.

Allying himself with humanism, Nagel advocates disciplined reason as the only instrument we have for achieving human goods. Since humanity is a product of this world, and not of a supernatural force, we must accept responsibility for our destiny and maximize the potential of natural and social resources.[14] Although humanistic naturalism in the Renaissance was closely allied with the study of Greek culture, its modern expression is more directly dependent on science.[15] Humanistic naturalism should not be confused with the other forms of humanism supported by great religious traditions, such as Judaism and Christianity.

Naturalism and the Educative Process
In accord with its metaphysical picture of reality, naturalism in education holds that the aim of education is to produce persons who are adjusted to the realities of the material world. Since science is the chief method for dealing with the physical world, it should be employed in formulating appropriate instructional procedures. According to a naturalistic scenario, students will be taught to exercise rational control over the physical world and enabled to fulfill their capabilities as natural agents. The results of a naturalistic education are people who lead orderly lives, draw accurate conclusions from observations of nature and human affairs, deal effectively with the environment and find appropriate expression for their natural abilities.

This naturalistic scheme makes the focus of the school curric-

ulum physical objects and the order they exhibit. Some naturalists think we can discover causal laws built into the universe.
Others are not so confident but believe that we can observe and
record regular sequences of events. In either case the basic ideas
of the cosmos are most clearly contained in physics, chemistry,
biology, zoology, astronomy, geology and other natural or
"hard" sciences. These studies should be at the core of the curriculum. Mathematics is also very important, because it is a precise language system for dealing with quantity and relationships
in the material realm.

Naturalists in education typically say that subjects such as
psychology, sociology, economics and other social sciences are
desirable to the extent that they avoid excessive speculation and
concentrate on formulating statistical generalizations or empirical laws. Some naturalists minimize the importance of literature, philosophy, art and the like because they do not involve
hard facts. Yet other naturalists see the humanities, at whatever
level of learning, as expressions of our human creativity and thus
make a place for them in the curriculum.

Whereas the naturalistic view of reality influences the shape of
the curriculum, its general view of knowledge affects preferences
for teaching and learning. Since the tangible world is the fundamental reality and sense perception is the basic way of knowing it, teachers should emphasize classroom demonstrations, laboratory experiments, field trips, audiovisual aids, object lessons
and other "sensory" methods of instruction. Teaching by direct
experience demands that the teacher master the principles of the
natural world so that he or she can properly select the learning
situations in which they can be disclosed. Most naturalists hold
that students should be initiated into the scientific method or
rational manner of problem-solving. Thinking scientifically is
often seen as the paradigm case of how persons can employ their
rationality as a tool for handling the natural environment.

Naturalism primarily envisions the teacher as an agent for

putting the students in touch with the world of facts. Naturalists who are also humanists see the teacher as assisting students in developing their own natural abilities. Unlike the idealist teacher, whose chief responsibility is to model appropriate personality and character traits, the naturalist teacher is often pictured as refraining from imposing his or her value judgments on the subject matter. In a sense teachers are to be neutral mediums through which the student contacts the real natural world.

B. F. Skinner is one of the most important naturalists to develop an approach to teaching and learning. Although Skinner is primarily a psychologist, his underlying philosophical assumptions are naturalistic. Skinner rejects the traditional conception that psychology is a study of an immaterial mind or self. Since such entities lack physical, observable dimensions, they are irrelevant to scientific investigation. He conceives of psychology, then, as the science of human behavior, the description of what external conditions produce specific responses.

Skinner wants to base education on the technology of behavior. He applies his findings about the reinforcement of responses in animals to the teaching-learning situation.[16] Without reference to "inner states" (for example, motives, intentions and volitions), Skinner asserts that desired behaviors can be brought about by arranging the conditions of reinforcement. The current educational scene shows signs of Skinner's emphasis on overt behavior: teaching machines have been constructed; performance objectives have been introduced into instructional planning; and competency-based teacher education has been made a standard for certification.

Obviously, behavior engineering offers more than a means of developing skills and imparting information. It provides a methodology which can shape many areas of student behavior, including ethical responses. However, Skinner refuses to prescribe what sorts of performances are desirable or what kind of individuals ought to be developed. He thinks that society must decide on the ideal person it wants to produce with the technology of teaching. The behaviorists simply offer effective ways to obtain the desired performances.

Of course, some naturalists are willing to state a general theory of value and draw its implications for education. Some naturalists believe that moral education should present the child with the lessons of the natural world in order to engender right conduct. At the elementary level, moral intuitions about the love of life might be fostered by showing the young the habits of robins caring for their babies in the nest. The virtue of patience might be taught by letting the children observe that, in many natural processes, time is needed to obtain results. Growing plants or becoming aware of the gestation periods of the animals can have this effect.

In more advanced forms moral education can proceed to abstract judgments about the natural world. Studying the complexity of the physical order, observing the economy of natural processes and even scrutinizing the dispositions of individuals and cultures can supply insight into the nature of things. When naturalists generalize about the proper ethical theory they frequently turn toward utilitarianism. Utilitarianism recognizes no absolute or universal values but defines right action as that which produces the greatest good for the greatest number of people. But the concept of what is good can vary from society to society.

Moral education for the naturalist is more than mere insight or proper motivation. It is ultimately connected with practical activity. Therefore, moral educators must inculcate desirable tendencies and dispositions in students. Harry Broudy explains:

> We want our children to develop reliable tendencies to tell the truth, to respect the codes of right and wrong of the community, to be courageous, to be persevering in the face of obstacles, to withstand the temptations of disapproved pleasures, to be able to sacrifice present pleasures in favor of more remote ones, to have a sense of justice and fair play.[17]

Such tendencies are seen by the naturalist to be in accord with the order of things. There is no need to justify these traits by a scale of absolute values; we only need to see that society generally approves them.

In teaching art and aesthetic appreciation, most naturalists stress the primacy of form and balance, as these elements are intrinsic to the natural process. Beauty in art pertains to its representation of some aspect of nature. The naturalist who teaches aesthetic appreciation employs hands-on experience or immediate sensory contact with various art media. Hence, whereas the idealist emphasizes abstract understanding of art, the naturalist stresses getting the feel of art by direct involvement.

The naturalist would wish to have younger students, say, fingerpaint or keep a simple beat with an instrument in order to gain a sense of the dynamics of painting or music. Older students might be asked to write and produce a drama or play an instrument in order to acquire appreciation for theater or music. By gaining a sense of technique or the importance of physical control or the ability to combine colors, a basis is established for the student to develop a taste for what constitutes greatness in these arts.

Among the wide spectrum of naturalists, there are those radical critics of modern education who say that it must be completely overhauled. Karl Marx insisted that Western culture's systems of schooling are instruments of class domination rather than means of liberating and enhancing our human abilities.[18] Following Marx's materialist analysis of history, his followers say that while there is free, public or state education, its character is determined by the structure of industrial, capitalistic society. Marxists, for example, protest the middle-class orientation of the public school in America because it links educational opportunity to economic status. The increasing documentation of these facts in educational sociology gives weight to their charge. We know all too well the plight of the black child in the slums; and we have learned that the economic class of students largely determines the amount of education they will receive and the life work they will pursue.

Marx's ideal is genuinely free and equal educational opportunity for all children. The content of this education should not perpetuate the notion that ideas are prior to actions and that theory is more important than practice. This notion, which reflects class distinctions, appears to justify giving an intellectual education to some and a vocational education to others. Moreover, the form of education should not be the transmission of static content to be absorbed.

For Marx, education should combine theoretical and practical activities, being and doing. It should recognize the active, dynamic nature of knowing. In this way education will no longer contribute to human alienation but will bring about persons who find dignity in their labor.

Of course Marxists believe that the ills of present education cannot be completely cured until society itself undergoes fundamental economic restructuring, until this period of capitalism gives way to socialism. Insofar as the working class can gain influence in the current educational scene, they should use it to help usher in the new era. However, Marx believed that the hope of educational liberalism, that all needed social changes can be effected through cooperative and nonviolent political action, is naive.[19]

Evaluating Naturalism

Naturalism, particularly in its more humanistic forms, must be respected for its emphasis on distinctively human qualities. Furthermore, naturalism correctly endorses the scientific method as a procedure for solving problems. And most versions of naturalism are willing to face the hard facts of the universe with courage and determination. Finally, the naturalist's faith that creative intelligence can actually improve our world is admirable.

Yet it is difficult to see how naturalism can adequately explain certain aspects of the reality we experience. For example, Nagel's view of the existence of physical objects and their properties may seem easy to understand, but it is difficult to accept that physical stuff is the sum total of reality. Mind and rational thought are not explicable in exclusively physical terms. Such realities seem to be different in kind from physical things and hence demand a different kind of explanation.

Nagel's position on the causal operations of matter runs the risk of determinism. C. S. Lewis argues that the view that all occurrences are physically caused has difficulty accounting for the existence of rational thought. He contends that thought is invalidated if it is produced by physical causes. One would ordinarily presume that a belief is rational only if it is held on the basis of evidence and logic. The irony which Lewis notes is damaging: if naturalism really is true, then the belief that it is true cannot be rationally held.[20]

Nagel's position on the primacy of matter and material forces also encounters the problem of making sense of free, responsible action. If human choices and actions are ultimately generated by brute, impersonal causes, then it is problematic explaining how they can be significantly free. The deterministic character of Marxist materialism is also troublesome because it posits historical or economic forces as causing all events.

The issue of value reveals another example of naturalism's impoverished attempt to explain important features of the world. Nagel, for example, denies that anything is intrinsically good or evil. Values, for him, are simply tentative hypotheses for guiding people in the exercise of their interests. Yet, in the end, some value must be assumed good for its own sake. With Nagel's position the obvious place to start is the issue of why we have any obligation to perform actions which maximize human interests. Either the value of maximizing human interests is fundamental or it is derived from some value which is. But it is ludi-

crous for Nagel to think that nothing is fundamentally good and
that we can still have ethical norms. One who says that nothing
is intrinsically good will unwittingly assume that something is.
So, as scientific as Nagel tries to be about ethics, his theory is
as prone to sentimentality, selectivity and projection as the idealistic position he rejects.

The philosophy of education associated with naturalism correctly recognizes the importance of learning by direct observation and practical experience. The emphasis on empirical inquiry
as the sole source of knowledge, however, is disproportionate.
Nagel admits that there are other ways of experiencing the universe than by knowing it, but insists that the only mode of real
knowledge is empirical. This position ignores the fact that different areas of intellectual activity have a legitimacy of their own
and encounter difficulty only when forced to meet criteria which
are foreign to their subject matters. Metaphysics, theology and
aesthetics are such disciplines.

A potential problem with some naturalistic theories of instruction is their reliance on conditioning and socialization techniques. These methods have been touted for producing not only
academic but ethical performance. Admittedly, scientists like
Skinner have identified significant similarities between human
beings and other animals, even in the way our responses can be
guided and controlled. It may be that these similarities can be
used in one phase of training children, particularly during early
years when reflective thought is minimal and some conditioning
is required.

But there is a danger. At worst, behavior engineering can be
manipulative and can damage the capacity for self-direction. An
exclusively behavioristic approach to moral training focuses on
publicly observable behavior and may reduce the student's ability
to act on the basis of principles and proper motives.[21] When one
adds to this difficulty the trouble naturalism has in designating
ends for moral and social life, grave concern arises over its ability

to provide a moral education.

Naturalism's theological inadequacy stems from its twofold rejection of nonempirical realities. Naturalistic metaphysics holds that nonempirical reality does not exist and typical naturalistic epistemology denies that nonempirical realities can be known. This undermines Christian claims about God and the Bible's ability to communicate theological truth.

Naturalistic philosophy opposes any theological position which affirms the reality of a deity or a supernatural dimension to reality. For Christianity, God is the eternal, sovereign Creator of the universe. He is not part of the physical world and yet he is present within it as Redeemer and Lord. For naturalism, the physical system is all that there is. The view of Nagel, Marx and other naturalists that humanity is purely a product of material elements conflicts with the biblical picture that human nature is created in the image of God.

While naturalism agrees with Christianity in affirming the reality and worth of nature, it is wrong in asserting the primacy of nature. Naturalism's insistence that physical nature must be known by empirical means is in accord with the understanding of most Christians. However, naturalism errs in holding that empirical investigation is the only way of gaining knowledge.

Neo-Thomism: Being and Essence

Like Aristotle, Thomas Aquinas held that only individual things are real.[22] For Thomistic philosophy, the fundamental concept is being or existence. A particular is real because it has being or existence. Objects of all kinds would be purely potential without the "act of being" to make them actual.

Unlike idealists who attribute existence to pure ideas and naturalists who recognize only the reality of matter, Aquinas says that the nature of a thing is a union of form and matter—an aspect which makes it understandable and an aspect which makes it tangible. But Aquinas adds that the nature or "essence" of a given thing must also be combined with "being"; *what* something is must be combined with the fact *that* it is.

Aquinas calls existence actuality and essence potentiality. Particular things are unities of actuality and potentiality. That is, every particular thing has a measure of reality and the capability to change in certain ways. Change occurs in the temporal world when some potentiality in a thing becomes actual.[23]

In the grand structure of reality everything has a definite nature or essence. Furthermore, Aquinas sees reality as a hierarchy with things arranged according to essence and existence. On the ladder of existence—from stones at the bottom, through oysters and complex animals, on to humans and angels near the top— all things possess a proportion of essence and existence. No finite thing has full actuality with no potentiality; no creature is free of limitation and dependency. At the top of the scale of reality is Pure Being. This is God in whom essence and existence are identical: his very nature is to exist. God is full actuality with no potentiality. In turn he is the source and fountainhead of all other existence. Aquinas believed that this way of understanding the Supreme Being provides a philosophical route to the God of Christianity, the great "I am."

The world picture of Thomism is a purposive one: the universe is moving toward a destiny. The divinely created natures of things tend toward fulfillment. The "end" of each object is built into its make-up. The process of moving toward an end is a manifestation of the potentiality-actuality structure of reality. Each existing kind of object seeks to actualize its unique potential.

In this overall scheme of the universe, the nature of humanity is a composite unity of the animal and the rational. Human beings share many physical characteristics with the animal kingdom. We must accommodate the needs and drives of the physical domain, and we share in some of its physical goods and pleasures. Yet the real uniqueness of our humanity lies in our rational and spiritual nature.

The epistemology of Thomism rests on its metaphysics. Since reality is a rationally structured system and the human mind is by nature rational, we are capable of knowing reality. The innate drive of the mind is to apprehend truth. The stable, orderly reality we inhabit accommodates that drive. As Mortimer Adler puts it, "the human mind naturally tends to learn, to acquire knowledge, just as the earth naturally tends to support vegetation."[24]

For the Neo-Thomist there are different kinds of knowing. There is sense experience which leads to revisable, scientific knowledge (for example, that there are nine planets in our solar system). And there is intuition which leads to unchangeable knowledge (for example, that every event has a cause). Truths evident to the senses comprise ordinary, day-to-day knowledge. But the more important type of knowledge is that which is self-evident, gained ultimately by rational insight or intuition.

In addition to sense perception and intuition, Aquinas recognizes revelation as a source of knowledge. Whereas the former two sources are active, the latter is relatively passive. In perception and intuition the human intellect is actively pursuing truth, but revelation comes through God's initiative to the receptive human mind. One can learn by revelation truths which could also be found by reason (such as the existence of God). But one can also learn by revelation truths which cannot be acquired by reason (such as the Trinitarian structure of the Godhead). Aquinas believes that the truths delivered by reason and revelation are compatible; the truths of revelation do not supplant or contradict those of reason.

Neo-Thomistic metaphysics governs the area of axiology as much as it does epistemology. The potentiality-actuality principle and the hierarchical arrangement of reality permeate the Neo-Thomistic position in both ethics and aesthetics. Just as human nature seeks truth, it also seeks goodness and beauty.

This does not mean that every person is in fact good or creates beauty. It means that there is a tendency in all humans toward these values, a potential which strives to become actual. Furthermore, the principle of hierarchy, which states that some objects have existence in greater measure than others, prioritizes the kinds of goodness and beauty in the world. The role of the rational agent, then, is to understand the hierarchical pattern of things good and beautiful, and to align his or her activities with them.

In ethics, goodness flows from the proper activity of reason. The morally good act is that which is controlled by the intellect. Knowledge of what is right is fundamental: people cannot do the right unless they know what it is. Cooperating with the intellect in the moral venture is the human will. The will is to perform what the intellect judges to be right. In Aquinas's conception of the moral life, the will is subservient to the intellect. Moral error, then, stems from either ignorance on the part of the intellect or weakness on the part of the will. The two problems of moral development, then, are helping the intellect to know what is right and getting the will to do it.

The intellect knows what is good by understanding the objective values inherent in reality. Commenting on the Thomistic ethical system, William McGucken identifies three areas of moral obligation, which are, in ascending order, duties to oneself, fellow human beings and God. He indicates that within these broad divisions there are more specific duties.[25] The values in this system are not contingent on human preferences but on the nature of reality.

Although modern people do not readily associate art with reason, Aquinas and his philosophical descendants make reason central to aesthetics. Jacques Maritain represents this view:

> Creativity, or the power of engendering, does not belong only to material organisms, it is a mark and privilege of life in spiritual things also. . . . The intellect in us strives to engender.

It is anxious to produce, not only the inner word, the concept, which remains inside us, but a work at once material and spiritual like ourselves, and into which something of our soul overflows. Through a natural super-abundance the intellect tends to express and utter outward, it tends to sing, to manifest itself in a work.[26]

So Neo-Thomists not only emphasize reason in art but also believe that human beings naturally tend toward the creation of beauty.

Maritain holds that aesthetic creativity is manifested in two areas, the fine arts and the practical arts. In the fine arts (music, painting, sculpture and so on) beauty is created for its own sake, purified of all extraneous elements. In the sphere of practical art (weaving, pottery and so on) useful objects are made pleasing or beautiful to the intellect. Thus their utility combines with aesthetic enjoyment. Since the practical arts have purposes in addition to the pure enjoyment of beauty, they are inferior to the fine arts.

In both areas of art the creative intellect attempts to express itself. The key concept in aesthetic judgments is that of excellence. Maritain says that "beauty delights the intellect . . . because it essentially means a certain excellence in the proportion of things to the intellect."[27] Among the more specific criteria for judging excellence are integrity, proportion and clarity.

Neo-Thomism and the Educative Process

For the Neo-Thomist, the world is a logically ordered system laden with value. It is the purpose of humanity to know the principles which pertain to that system. Curriculum proposals are readily forthcoming. The ecclesiastical wing of Neo-Thomism (represented by such thinkers as Jacques Maritain and John Henry Newman) includes subjects in the curriculum which deal with theistic themes and Christian doctrines. Historically this kind of emphasis gave foundation to the Catholic parochial educational establishment. The lay Neo-Thomists (represented by Mortimer Adler and Robert Hutchins) do not give such primacy to the religious dimension of the curriculum and endorse subjects which exhibit the absolute truths of the cosmos (such as logic, mathematics and languages) and the enduring themes of human nature (the humanities, for example).

The Neo-Thomist theory of knowledge is rich with directives about how teaching and learning should take place. According to Maritain, the ultimate goal of education is to develop our essential nature as human beings.[28] Since he considers the mind to be the core of human nature, Maritain says education is primarily the nurturing of the intellect. Teaching ideas, imparting facts and reinforcing good habits are some methods which can be used to achieve this end, but it is ultimately what transpires in the inner sanctum of the person that matters most.

The aim of all pedagogical methods is to increase the power of the student's mind. The basic goal is to teach all subjects so that the mind of the learner becomes able to see general principles and logical connections and thus acquires a knowledge of true reality. For the task of training the intellect, the formal discipline of education is as important as its content. A disciplined mind has the ability to handle life's situations, including the need for continued learning. Although Neo-Thomists are noted for stressing the disciplinary aspect of education, Maritain insists on creating for students a climate of freedom, creativity and love.

Maritain's moral theory makes the intellect and will primary factors in moral education.[29] Reason must develop the ability to deliver proper moral evaluations. Understanding moral laws and applying them to concrete situations are skills which must be learned. Moreover, complete moral education requires that the will be disciplined to follow the judgments of reason.

Although Maritain desires to use the best methods of training the will (approval-disapproval, reward-punishment and so on), he holds that responsible action flows from the inner wellspring of moral reason. Maritain assents to the doctrine of the Fall which asserts that both the intellect and the will are in a weakened condition. He argues, however, that enough of our natural endowment as moral beings remains intact to be educated and refined.

In aesthetic education, training the reason is also primary. Although many people associate the arts with the expression of feelings, Maritain holds that reason is intimately involved in the appreciation and creation of beauty. Hence the intellects of students must be prepared for aesthetically meaningful activity. Their minds must be brought to a point of clarity and sharpness by means of the customary disciplinary procedures.

When students have acquired basic content and techniques, the pedagogue can then cultivate the students' intuitive perceptions and creative drives. Their intuitive capability probes into the essence of the work of art and the creative capacity manifests their own inner nature. Maritain endorses both the contemplative and the productive sides of aesthetic activity.

Evaluating Neo-Thomism

In a sense, Neo-Thomism navigates between the two extremes of idealism and naturalism. Whereas idealism recognizes only mind as the basis of reality and naturalism recognizes only matter, Neo-Thomism affirms the dual aspects of reality. This is largely due to Aquinas's adoption of the Aristotelian system which conceives of particular things as unions of form and matter. Aquinas's Christian views, then, shape his explanation of the theistic dimension of reality.

One objection to the philosophy of St. Thomas is that a teleological universe has difficulty encompassing genuine human freedom. Some think that such a universe tends to operate automatically. Aquinas argues, however, that our distinct nature includes free choice, even the ability to choose to go against the moral order.

Aquinas's epistemology recognizes empirical experience and cognition of abstract truths. He holds that many truths originate in sense experience but are finally grasped conceptually. Thus he relates seemingly contradictory elements of divergent viewpoints without being eclectic or arbitrary.

The Thomistic view that there are universal values makes initial sense of our moral condition. Furthermore, the ethical theory of Thomism recognizes a relationship between the conceptual and empirical, the absolute and the relative. Aquinas believes that universal values, known conceptually, are capable of varying applications to concrete situations. By steering a middle course between legalism and situationism, this position suggests a healthy direction for moral education.

As a philosophy of education Neo-Thomism is an established movement, enjoying allegiance from the Roman Catholic side of Christianity. In its lay expression, however, Neo-Thomism has appeal for many thinkers in other segments of Christianity and even for some secular thinkers.

As a representative Neo-Thomist, Maritain would view the idealist's "imitation of the Absolute Mind" as romantic and the naturalist's "conformity to nature" as dehumanizing. He emphasizes developing the natural powers of the mind, that aspect of our being which makes us distinctively human. The premium placed on the cultivation of the mind, in all of its different functions, is noteworthy. It stems from the conviction that intelligent self-direction is the key to human dignity and achievement.

Maritain asserts that the benefits of knowledge and personal freedom can be gained only through discipline and diligence. Being more completely in the classic natural law tradition than the naturalist, Maritain does not accept just the disciplinary and pedagogical methods based on laws of our animal nature. He also embraces educational procedures which reflect our rational understanding of enduring values.

Some critics argue that Neo-Thomist educators are committed to the "calisthenics theory of learning" and the "spinach theory of education." The calisthenics image suggests that students learn by the arduous drill of their faculties and that a dominating teacher plays the role of leading the mental drills. The spinach image suggests that if the intellect and character are shaped through toughening the powers of self-discipline, then whatever is unpleasant to do in school can be used to develop them. Winston Churchill, probably with tongue in cheek, once said, "It doesn't much matter what you teach a boy, so long as he doesn't enjoy it." At its extreme, this view leads one to think that the most distasteful subjects must be the most beneficial and therefore must be given high priority.

Needless to say, some educators, both Neo-Thomist and otherwise, have held such unacceptable views. However, it is a distortion to saddle Maritain and most Neo-Thomists with such stereotypes. Maritain's emphasis on the dignity of the human spirit is commendable, as is his recognition that educational good comes only with intellectual work. Besides, Maritain clearly advocates encouraging the creative and free expressions of children and thinks that their sheer delight with proper education helps them actualize their potential. He specifies that in educational transactions the student is the primary agent and the teacher is secondary.[30]

In relationship to Christianity, the philosophy of Aquinas raises several important issues. Its metaphysical picture of the world, which posits God and the hierarchically ordered creation, is a respectable Christian theory of reality. Yet some Christian thinkers believe that Greek thought forms, which Aquinas borrowed largely from Aristotle, distort rather than clarify biblical ideas. These thinkers argue that classical metaphysics makes God static and impersonal rather than dynamic and personal, pure being with no room for becoming.[31]

The epistemology of Aquinas and Neo-Thomists such as Maritain accents rationality and the primacy of truth, presenting a feasible Christian version of human knowing. However, some critics fear that it leads to an overly intellectualistic approach to faith. The moral theory of Thomas Aquinas and his followers, which stresses the objective character of values, also reflects some basic Christian understandings. Yet certain critics think that it fallaciously gives priority to being over doing and theory over practice.

3

Contemporary
Philosophies
of Education

*T*raditional philosophical per-
spectives, no matter how divergent in substance and detail, share
a common assumption: the human mind can know the nature of
reality. Idealism, naturalism and Neo-Thomism hold that the
role of philosophy is to build a comprehensive view of life and
the world. Although it is rather unusual in contemporary
thought, this approach to philosophy still attracts a number of
thinkers.

In the past several hundred years radical changes have oc-
curred in the way philosophy is conceived and practiced. From
René Descartes's posture of doubt to David Hume's skeptical
challenges, the traditional confidence in our most basic beliefs
has eroded. Even the existence of oneself and of the external
world are sometimes thought to need proof. Immanuel Kant
dealt another blow to the traditional role of philosophy by claim-

ing that metaphysics is a kind of mental projection, not a science of objective reality.

As modern forces continued to destroy confidence in our ability to build a comprehensive view of reality, a number of philosophical perspectives developed. Most notably, experimentalism, existentialism and philosophical analysis came on the scene. Although they profess not to have a systematic view of reality, knowledge and value, each one makes implicit assumptions about such matters. This chapter discusses the basic perspective of each position and shows how it affects philosophy of education.

It is not difficult to uncover assumptions linked to an underlying world view in experimentalism and existentialism. However, analytic philosophy, which is essentially a method, tries to avoid making many assumptions. Philosophers with quite divergent philosophical positions use analytic procedures.

Experimentalism: Experience and Society

As an established philosophy, experimentalism (sometimes called pragmatism or instrumentalism) is less than a century old. Experimentalism rejects any concept of a transcendent or ultimate reality (for example, the idealist's realm of ideas and supreme mind, the Aristotelian's pure form, the Neo-Thomist's absolute being). The experimentalist believes that common human experience is the only basis for philosophy and charges that all traditional, otherworldly views rest on metaphysical presumption.

As John Dewey has explained, the realm of "experience" does not pertain simply to sense experience; it encompasses all that human beings do and think and feel, from passive reflection to active doing. He held that this world of human experience is adequate for the fulfillment of human purposes and the satisfaction of human understanding. For Dewey, whatever lies beyond the world of ordinary experience is unknowable.

Dewey's emphasis on the world of ordinary experience is distinct from the traditional realist position, such as the Neo-Thomist would hold. Traditional realism asserts that there is an objective reality to which our beliefs should conform and that our epistemic processes are well adapted for this purpose. Dewey, however, settles for experience as the very reality we seek and therefore tries to avoid a dualism between the objective world and subjective belief.

It is not merely the subject-object dualism which is collapsed by experimentalism. John Childs explains that in experience all dichotomies melt away:

> The divisions between the natural and the supernatural, the real and the ideal, reality and appearance, subject and object, mind, body, thought and activity, all seem to many to be obviously natural dualisms. . . . [The] experimentalist . . . asserts unqualifiedly that experience is all that we have. . . . Hence, if human experience cannot give us an adequate account of realities, then man has no possibility of gaining such an account.[1]

When Dewey insists on experience as the ultimate ground of human discourse, he means that it is the only sure measure of whether our ideas are true.

Dewey conceives of human experience as the collective experience of human beings, not as the private, inner feelings of isolated individuals. Private experience can be corrected by the shared experience of those living in society. That is, whatever claims one makes about "reality" may be looked at by all and checked out in the realm of experience which is open to community inspection. According to Dewey the "reality of experience" is in continual flux and flow. Experience, and therefore reality, is in constant process.

In contrast to intellectually oriented epistemologies, Dewey offers an experientially oriented one. Since reality is characterized by experiential change, knowledge is temporary and tentative. Knowledge is not an item for passive contemplation, but an instrumentality for solving problems and managing the ever-changing world. The test of some hypothesis or claim is whether, when put into practice, it really "works." To the degree that it is practicable, it can be said to be true. Public consensus about what works in certain human situations or what best solves empirical problems is the sole criterion of truth.

Experience, as Dewey says, has a "transactional" character, which means that human beings are in a great dialectic with their world. People develop through raw experience certain ideas and hunches about the way things are. They act on these ideas and then undergo their consequences. Depending on how things turn out, people revise their initial hypotheses. Dewey describes the "complete act of thought" from a perceived difficulty in the flow of events, through subsequent diagnosis and inventory of possible solutions, to testing for consequences of proposed solutions.[2] Dewey's controlled transaction is simply the layperson's version of the method of science.

Dewey applies scientific methodology to ethical and aesthetic questions, rejecting the notion that we must search for moral absolutes in some transcendent realm. He insists that we must explore the questions of value in the very place where people in fact do their valuing: within the boundaries of experience.

According to Dewey, ethical values are not discovered but constructed. Risky business though it is, human beings still have to create values and make normative claims without transcendental help. They have to make revisable, temporary recommendations about what is good or right. Ethical proposals express a longing to rearrange experience, or specific features of experience, in a more desirable way.

So the traditional question "What ought I to do?" becomes for Dewey an invitation to designate certain ends or purposes as desirable and then to try them out to see if the ensuing events lead us to retain or revise them. Again, the dictum "What works is good" does not refer merely to what works for the individual, but to what works for the community. Actions which seem to bring "good" to the individual, such as lying and stealing, have negative effects in the wider society and hence are not really good. For Dewey, the ultimate test of values is adaptation to the social and physical environment.

Dewey's aesthetic views also revolve around the concept of experience. He holds that a work of art is not a special type of entity or object which produces a specific effect in us. Rather the work of art is a catalyst for changing the experience of those who take it seriously. The dynamic, experiential consequences of a work of art provide the measure of its aesthetic worth. Experimentalists characterize earlier philosophies as looking for some objective standard beyond the world of human beings, but see themselves as locating the criterion of artistic value in how people feel or respond.

The task of the artist is to acquire new insights, experiences, feelings and intuitions—and stimulate those same reactions in us. Dewey writes, "Every art communicates because it expresses. It enables us to share vividly and deeply in meaning to which we had been dumb. . . . Communication is the process of creating participation, of making common what had been isolated and singular."[3] The democratic tone of experimentalist aesthetics allows common citizens to acclaim something a true work of art if in its presence they find new meanings to life, have new dimensions of feeling and, as a result, make better emotional contact with other people.

Experimentalism and the Educative Process

Ultimate reality, for the experimentalist, is social experience. It is the ever-changing collective feelings, hopes, problems and pains of the community. It is a realm in the dynamic process of becoming, what William James called "the universe with the lid off." Therefore, the school curriculum, which should be designed to reflect the nature of reality, must be a series of well-planned experiences in which the dynamic quality of our world is represented. The pedagogical task is not to impart bodies of static knowledge, usually broken into so many departments. Such a curriculum would give students an entirely fallacious impression of their world.

Dewey prefers "procedural" subjects to those which are "substantive." He regards studies which portray social life and problems as more important than those which examine nonhuman objects. Courses of study organized around procedures help students learn the manner in which to approach and solve the problems of life. Courses with socially oriented content enable students to get a feeling for the flux and flow of human experience.

Social studies would be a prime candidate for an experimentalist curriculum. Exploring current problems and issues tends to be favored over courses covering large blocks of established material. For example, courses on modern family living, peace studies and problems of Western democracy might be encouraged in the middle and high schools. Seminars on race relations, thermonuclear war, women's studies and changing sexual attitudes would be important in the college setting. Traditional courses in history or physics would be included because they are useful for understanding and managing our present world. As Morris and Pai say, "The entire curriculum will be inverted from subject matter intended to be applied later to life situations to the life situations themselves that provoke the kinds of learning in or between subject matter areas that intelligent living calls for."[4]

Rather than simply "tell" students that a certain situation or problem is interesting or important, Dewey suggests that the teacher try to arouse their sense of curiosity. Once aroused, it will carry the students through the planned course of study. According to this "learner-centered" approach, the teacher should cater to the interests of the students. Learning is likely to be richer and last longer if it stems out of the pupils' own needs and problems.

Dewey's theory of learning is not only problem-oriented and learner-centered, but also activity-based. The problems identified by the learner's interest must be actively approached. Learners must get involved with whatever topic or problem they select and must learn its characteristics as well as the general skills of problem solving. In short, we learn by doing. The traditional, logical method of pedagogy presents a systematic, organized body of material ("predigested"). The psychological method, however, links the subject to the learner's life situation and then lets him or her work through ("digest") it in initially chaotic form until a clearer understanding emerges. Dewey advises teachers to resist the "strong temptation to assume that presenting subject matter in its perfected form provides a royal road to learning."[5]

A logical approach to teaching geography might begin with the earth as a planet in our solar system, and then proceed to an explanation of the seasons and climates around the globe. Next the land and water masses, the Northern and Southern Hemispheres, and the physical characteristics of the various continents could be discussed. Later, the study might focus on the United States, its regions and its climate, its flora and fauna, and eventually the student's home state or town. A psychological approach would virtually reverse the traditional sequence of study, beginning with the learner's own location and moving outward to larger geographical entities as the student's interest naturally expands.

The experimentalist emphasis on society and community is evident in Dewey's view of value education, character building and the cultivation of aesthetic taste. Dewey does not appeal to some abstract standard to determine our values, but to communally accepted ideals and norms. The values which society endorses are best taught through experience. Children, indeed all people, learn what they live. The fabric of real life—with all of its problems and pressures, its interests and satisfactions—is a better catalyst for learning than purely didactic instruction.

In ethical and aesthetic education, then, the experimentalist educator must aid the group in identifying problem situations, experimenting with solutions and their consequences, and letting the disposition of the majority have sway. The emphasis on values being shaped by group preferences should operate in situations ranging from the school playground, where young children learn that it is better to take turns on the seesaw than to allow bullies to wrest seats from the weaker pupils, to a graduate program, where students realize that cooperative research is more productive than splintered, competitive efforts.

According to Dewey, science helps us determine areas of social agreement. On empirical, practical grounds—apart from metaphysical pronouncements and sectarian dogma—we can find unity about what is right and wrong, good and bad. Morris and Pai write,

> It is this possibility of a kind of nonmetaphysical, nontheistic, wholly secular brotherhood that some people feel is most nearly realized in the free, universal, secular public school in America. It is the "melting pot" idea expanded to include not only language and custom and style of dress but basic beliefs and life values.[6]

Moreover, if what students find to be the most workable morality is at variance with that of the larger society, then the teacher may recommend that the pupils assume some responsibility in changing the prevailing social pattern. Hence the school has a greater duty than merely the inculcation of existing social practice. Its function is the intelligent criticism of the public standard.

In the matter of aesthetic values and the cultivation of taste, Dewey again relies on the socialized approach. Rather than fos-

ter deeply private intuitions or radically divergent artistic sentiments among students, the experimentalist tries to expose them
to what society deems appropriate. The experimentalist teacher
will try to encourage students to get involved in the whole aesthetic venture, to make some aesthetic judgments, to take hold
of various media, to try to create art, and so forth. The ultimate
purpose of aesthetic education is not merely to get students to
approve the classic works of art, so to speak, but to allow them
to find fuller dimensions of meaning within their individual and
social lives.

Evaluating Experimentalism

With its emphasis on technology and satisfactory consequences,
experimentalism expresses the mood of contemporary American
and Western European life. If we accept the attitude that life can
be improved, then we are more likely to work toward and achieve
a better world. Furthermore, the pragmatic emphasis on democracy, human freedom and certain forward-looking social move-
ments must be applauded.

A problem with Dewey's version of experimentalism is his
claim that the nature of reality is beyond human grasp. But no
philosophical position can get off the ground without tacitly
positing at least a rough and general picture of what reality is
like. Thus Dewey's talk about the world-as-experienced simply
replaces more traditional candidates for prime reality with a new-
er candidate. Moreover, Dewey's "naturalization" of experience
is very naturalistic. So his position does not avoid making assumptions about the way the world is; it simply refuses to pay
sufficient attention to the genuine metaphysical issues which
inevitably arise for all philosophical views.

Truth, for experimentalism, is always relative to some individual or group. Dewey says that whatever ideas enable us to ma-
neuver effectively in the world are "true." Yet we cannot expect
the things that were true for people in medieval times to be true

for moderns. Our changing experience causes us to change the ideas we need for dealing with life. As William James says, "True ideas are those that we can assimilate, validate, corroborate and verify. False ideas are those that we can not."[7] So the notion that there are propositions which are true about the way the world is, independently of what people think about the matter, is rejected.

One of the easiest criticisms of Dewey's theory of knowledge is to subject it to its own relativism, saying that it may be true for some people, but not for others. A more substantial criticism would be that it is not clear that the test of truth as "workability" readily applies to certain significant areas of truth. Logical and mathematical truths, for example, seem to be independent of what people think and thus elude experimentalist efforts to relativize all knowledge.

Stroll and Popkin rehearse a standard appraisal of the pragmatic orientation of Dewey and others:

> Some have contended that "working" is too vague a concept, and, as a result, that it is difficult, if not impossible, to determine whether an idea or a belief has "worked." If ideas and beliefs are to be evaluated in terms of whether their consequences "work" out satisfactorily in experience, how does one determine the possible consequences in order to test ideas and beliefs?[8]

Potential outcomes branch off in many directions and are virtually infinite in number. They also reach indefinitely into the future, making a thorough test of them very difficult.

In Dewey's ethical theory, standards of morality become relativized and popularized: what is right for one person or society can be wrong for another, depending on their different experiences. However, this line of thinking makes a fundamental mistake: while each person or group has a particular perspective on ethics, it does not follow that there are no universal principles of morality. Although changing situations demand different applications of moral principles, Dewey has failed to show that fundamental moral obligations are subject to changeable group opinion and experience.[9]

Dewey's view of beauty and aesthetic taste has particular problems. While Dewey is correct to emphasize the need for art (beautiful objects and pleasing experiences) to be available to a wide public, he is mistaken to think that the public can set the standard for what is beautiful. Dewey basically says that beauty is what people enjoy, that what is admired ought to be admired. He rejects the notion that a work of art can have a certain intrinsic excellence which is admirable regardless of whether it is enjoyed in common society. His failure to distinguish between enjoyable and admirable beauty in aesthetics is parallel to his failure to distinguish relative and absolute factors in morality.[10]

The educational implications of Dewey's philosophy have been quite controversial. This is certainly true of the basic claim of his experimentalism: the student is one who experiences and hence the immediate experience of the student must be addressed. Who could deny that stirring the interest, arousing the curiosity, and inviting the participation of the student is desirable? But a danger is that the student can get the impression that he or she is the center of the educational enterprise, almost an autonomous agent in the schooling process. It is possible, then, that this orientation can lead students to be too egocentric, preoccupied with their own immediate needs and desires to the extent that they fail to understand and appreciate a larger perspective on human life and history.[11]

Another intriguing difficulty in Dewey's educational thinking arises regarding his belief that the school is to be both the mirror of society—a prime agent in the socialization process—and a constructive critic of society—a catalyst for needed change. Dewey's general philosophy accents the place of the social group in setting standards and expectations for individual behavior. Yet he often advocates that teachers help students become aware of those social forms which have negative results and urge them to try to change them as they assume their roles in society.[12] Two problems surface at this point. Dewey can identify no discernible agreement on values and goals in our diverse society. Neither can he justify importing the teacher's hidden agendas for moral and social progress into the classroom.

The naturalistic flavor of Dewey's experimentalism does not comport well with the Christian world view. Christianity affirms that the cosmos is created by a supreme spiritual being, governed by certain unchanging moral principles and made to be a kind of prelude to eternity. Experimentalist philosophy, by contrast, denies the existence of God, takes empirical things to exhaust reality, views all moral principles as revisable tools and rejects any conception of life after death. Other points of disagreement pertain to whether humankind is sinful and in need of redemption and whether miraculous divine intervention in the world is possible.

To their credit, Dewey and other experimentalists have discovered some important things about our creaturehood under God without realizing it. Christianity agrees with experimentalism that the need for human cooperation is paramount in learning and other enterprises. The democratic ideal, along with its vision for legitimate pluralism and respect among people, is certainly related to enlightened Christian thinking. Also, the idea that we are creatures who devise means to desired ends is a fact about the way God made us.

Although experimentalism is weak on theoretical grounds, its appeal is that many of its educational methods seem to work. A plausible explanation is that experimentalist methods (direct experience and problem solving, among others) rest on *some* facts about humanity, while experimentalist philosophy misunderstands the *full* meaning of human nature. A more adequate Christian account of humanity can endorse many of the same sorts of practical methods.

Existentialism: Individual and Choice

The hallmark of existentialism is its radical personalizing of the enduring questions of philosophy. The intellectual ancestry of existentialism is usually traced to Søren Kierkegaard and Friedrich Nietzsche in the nineteenth century. But most of the theoretical work, solidifying it into a major philosophical perspective, was done by European writers in this century.

The metaphysics of existentialism does not posit a fixed and absolute reality, such as the idealist's Mind or the naturalist's Nature. Existentialists tend to deny any rationality or order in the universe; everything is radically contingent. Existentialism focuses on the individual existing human being rather than the shared, social experience of experimentalism.

According to Jean Paul Sartre, human nature is basically undefined. In traditional metaphysical and theological systems, a universal or essence defines everything that exists. For Sartre there are no universals or pure essences by which we can understand the meaning of things, much less what we are as human beings. The classical view was that "essence precedes existence." Sartre explains that existentialism reverses the situation, declaring that "existence precedes essence." In other words, we first become aware *that* we are, that we exist: we did not ask to be born and yet we wake up one day to find out that we are here. From this starting point, we commence the long process of trying to fashion *what* we are, our essence: we create the meaning of our own lives. As Sartre writes, "Man is nothing but what he makes of himself."[13]

The chief characteristic of the individual is the necessity of making choices, the inescapable burden of choosing who I am and what I will be. Even those who search for answers in the will and plan of God, as religion offers, or in the principles of transcendental metaphysics, as idealism offers, must choose to accept or reject what is offered. And those who claim that questions about the ultimate meaning of life need not be addressed, as experimentalism holds, are thereby still making a choice.

On the issue of God's existence the existentialist movement is divided into theistic and atheistic camps. The theistic or religious wing looks to Kierkegaard as its fountainhead. Actually, we could find prototype existentialists as far back as Blaise Pascal and, in a certain sense, Socrates. Religious existentialism includes numerous contemporary figures: Gabriel Marcel, Karl Barth, Paul Tillich, Martin Buber and Jacques Ellul. The atheistic wing of existentialism draws much of its original inspiration from Friedrich Nietzsche. It claims Albert Camus and Jean Paul Sartre, among others, as modern representatives.

What differentiates theistic existentialism from traditional theism, and maintains its tie with atheistic existentialism, is its insistence on the tenuous nature of the human situation. Classical theistic theology and metaphysics affirm God's existence and perfect character as well as humanity's ability to know him. However, theistic existentialism starts at the same place that its sibling, atheistic existentialism, does: the aloneness and the riskiness of the human condition. We cannot know in any objective sense whether God really exists, but must exercise faith in him and live as if he exists. The "as if" posture of existentialist faith reminds us of our responsibility without specifying what our choices should be. Existential faith, then, is always perilous and never easy.

Atheistic existentialism prides itself in taking a stark but realistic view of the world in which we find ourselves, a world which does not include deity. Sartre explains:

The [atheistic] existentialist . . . thinks it very distressing that God does not exist, because all possibility of finding values in a heaven of ideas disappears along with Him. . . . Existentialism isn't so atheistic that it wears itself out showing that God doesn't exist. Rather, it declares that even if God did exist, that would change nothing. . . . Not that we believe that God exists, but we think that the problem of His existence is not the issue.[14]

The issue is our responsibility for personal choice.

According to Sartre, human civilization, supported by traditional philosophy, has emphasized the objective knowledge of things, quantity and data. The attempt to objectify all knowledge finds strong expression in the scientific method which began in the natural sciences, but is being extended in our day to the social sciences and behavioral sciences. This trend betrays the growing presumption that humanity—what it means to be human—can be known in the same way that atoms, machines and laboratory animals can be investigated. Sartre argues that we cannot attain self-knowledge or interpersonal knowledge in the same way we know things.

In discussing existentialist epistemology here, George Kneller says that "the validity of knowledge is determined by its value to the individual."[15] His remark amplifies Sartre's concept that meaning comes from within the individual. The concept of truth takes a somewhat different shape in the thought of Sartre and other existentialists. Under the traditional conception, propositions are true when they correspond to the way things really are. Sartre, however, expands the concept of truth, suggesting that the true is the real or the genuine. Hence, a person is a "true" person when he or she has cast off sham and superficiality, and has embarked on an earnest search for meaning and personal integrity.

Existentialists have been preoccupied with the theory of value broadly conceived. Sartre's writings on ethics and aesthetics emphasize the individual and the necessity of choice. The uncomfortable but inevitable matter of ethical decision arises in a specific way for Sartre. As an atheistic existentialist, he denies moral absolutes and any way of determining what proper morality is. If there were absolutes, and if we could know them with certainty, then we would lose our essential freedom as human beings As H. J. Blackham indicates, "My freedom is the unique foundation of values."[16] Theistic existentialists as well stress the inevitability of decision, although they envision a different fundamental decision about life.

Existentialists further argue that each choice becomes an element in the larger orientation of one's life. Implicit in every decision is an axiological assumption about the meaning and worth of human existence. Over the years of our lives, therefore, we actually construct our own picture of humankind, a definition of the person. Since we cannot escape having to reveal our values and shape the meaning to life by our cumulative choices, existentialists say we should face the whole business squarely and earnestly. Theistic existentialists are willing to build life on the human longing for an ultimate being, although they think it has no objective verification. Atheistic existentialists think that to be human in the noblest sense is to recognize our aloneness in the universe and the necessity of making moral decisions.

Rather than consult public consensus or transcendent principles for the standard of aesthetic taste, existentialism asserts that each individual must decide what is pleasing, delightful and beautiful. Traditional aesthetics derives the meaning of art from an objective world of things. The worth of a portrait, for example, would be determined by how well it represents the personage in question. Existentialists deny that art must be a replica of an external object, in either the empirical or ideal realm.

Existentialism provided powerful motivation for the development of nonrepresentationalist theories of art. In fact, under existentialist influence, works of art in music, painting and film deliberately violated or rejected prevailing modes of composition in order to make an "existentialist statement" about the human condition.[17] Their underlying theme was that art must personally "engage" both the artist and the recipient of art.

Existentialism and the Educative Process
Since existentialists recognize no fixed and unchanging reality,

their educational theorizing heads in an unconventional direction. Numerous existentialist writings bear either directly or indirectly on educational philosophy.

Sartre and other existentialists would have the subject matter of the curriculum include a heavy offering of courses which emphasize the elusive, inner recesses of personhood. Courses in the sciences and quantifiable data are of secondary importance to those invoking the selfhood of the student. The exact subjects of study and the materials for teaching them would be selected according to how well they elicit the student's "awareness of freedom and responsibility." Some existentialists who are less individualistic, such as Martin Buber, say that the awareness of freedom is the basis for interpersonal relationships.[18]

Sartre indicates that such subjects as the arts give opportunity for self-expression. Also, the social sciences provide occasions for the student to react to important issues and problems, and great literature can allow students to "feel their way" into the situation of another character and vicariously work through the relevant choices. While the preceding subjects are particularly helpful, any subject is acceptable as long as it provides the right conditions for individual reflection and decision. Van Cleve Morris says that the existentialist curriculum should intensify personal involvement.[19]

The courses in the existentialist curriculum are not viewed as static, prepackaged bodies of information. Genuine education is a dynamic process in which the student is brought to face his or her own existence. This means that all courses, and the total learning environment, must be constructed so that there are opportunities for attaining self-knowledge: individual decision, inward growth and ethical development.

The subjective takes precedence over the objective, since even seemingly secure truths about the objective world must be validated by the "I" which stands behind all believing and knowing. One must appropriate knowledge for oneself. Prevailing educational structures fail to recognize this, since they rest on the modern dichotomies between objective and subjective, thought and emotion, fact and value. This is why Sartre insists that we need serious revision in the way we learn, a revision which fosters personal wholeness.[20]

According to Kneller, the teaching approach which best corresponds to the type of learning the existentialists want is what we might call the "Socratic method."[21] The Socratic method for eliciting self-knowledge involves asking hard questions which may threaten the status quo and make the learner uncomfortable. Because they are always afraid that learners might retreat to a transcendental tradition or the group consensus, existentialist educators will devise ways to stir students into an awareness of their selfhood.

Sartre's axiology implies that moral and aesthetic education aim at individual involvement. The formation of character is accomplished by allowing students to discover their role as judge of what is valuable. They must realize that the teachings of absolutist theological or metaphysical systems are not binding on them, and that they alone must shoulder their responsibility, choose their values, and thus shape their lives. Sartre holds that we should not demand of anyone perfect compliance with any social system, set of beliefs or code of conduct. The child's moral development is a deeply private matter.

For existentialism, the refinement of aesthetic sensibility is a twofold process. First, it involves freeing children from traditional forms of production and criticism, and from the social pressure to feel and respond in certain ways. Second, it involves helping children to create art as their own statement about life and react to art in general on the basis of their own existential situations. Conformity to standing tradition and popularity with peers cannot be used as criteria for appraising an existentialist work of art. Sartre emphasizes the role of the imagination in art.[22] In order to help generate imaginative energy, many existentialist educators use a nondirective approach and encourage the construction of an environment which is open and sensitive to individual feelings.[23]

Evaluating Existentialism

The emphasis on the primacy of the individual is both the boon and bane of the existentialist movement. On the one hand, existentialism correctly beckons us to awaken to our responsibility as individual human beings. On the other hand, the precise way existentialist philosophy conceives of human selfhood is troublesome.

Sartre's idea that the cosmos is devoid of meaning and thus that one must shape one's own destiny is the beginning of philosophical peril. He holds that the individual must ultimately decide what is real and what is true. The insightful claim that the individual has to certify truth escalates quickly into the more radical thesis that individual choice creates reality and truth. When intellect is subordinated to will, the downward slide into pure arbitrariness is hard to avoid.

Excessive individualism can also be detected in Sartre's ethics and aesthetics. While the need for individual expression is not illegitimate, Sartre's emphasis is too egoistic, treating the individual's wants and needs as paramount. Particularly in ethics this position fails to explain the objective status we assign to ethical judgments. We not only tend to attribute objectivity to basic ethical principles, but cannot fathom how the concepts of duty and obligation, and of good and evil, make sense if they are founded wholly on individual willing. It is difficult for Sartre and other existentialists to argue that the act of choosing creates the value of what is chosen.

The implications of Sartre's position for educational philosophy are of mixed worth. Sartre's accent on individual appropriation is fundamental and excellent for the educational enterprise. Yet the desire for a minimum of structure and encouragement of extreme forms of self-expression can have negative educational results. Selfhood is discovered, to a degree, in dimensions of otherness—both the otherness of different persons and of an external environment. Existentialist prescriptions for self-development probably do not place sufficient stress on self-control, self-editing and self-giving in relation to others. A few existentialists (Buber is one) would develop educational thinking along more interpersonal lines.

The existential message for education can have devastating results. Focus on the individual, out of proportion to the corporate heritage of humanity, can erode interest in transmitting and improving civilization and culture. In the end, it can lead to the illusion that the individual is the center of the universe. The initial promise of total freedom and complete responsibility can result in profound unhappiness and melancholy. Actually, Sartre's concern for the inward, personal struggle for meaning resonates with Christian teachings on the nature of personhood. Historic Christianity affirms that humanity is made in the image of God and that this image involves a moral and spiritual aspect which longs for fulfillment. The radical flaw of sin in human life explains, in part, the difficulties in finding this fulfillment.

Certainly the Christian view of a fallen but needy humanity provides an understanding of why the world appears meaningless and absurd to the atheistic existentialist. If one looks to science or formal philosophy alone for the ultimate answer to human existence, without seeing the world which science and philosophy investigate as a creation of God, then one will be disappointed. When the world is elevated to the status of final answer, despair and desolation of the human spirit result. A Christian perspective departs from atheisic existentialism, then, in affirming that the world—understood as a creation of a supremely intelligent and loving Creator—is orderly and purposeful.

Much in Christianity also resonates with the theistic existentialist's call for total, unconditional commitment to God. However, the existential characterization of religious faith is problematic. Typically, existentialists say that reason is ineffectual in making religious commitments and that a passionate act of choice must decide matters. While recognizing the limitations of reason and the importance of faith has its point, the existentialist view excludes a vital aspect of our being from the most basic decisions of life.

Also, we may ask whether the typical existential description of faith as a subjective, volitional response can be salvaged from self-projection and wish fulfillment. Surely the eternal nature of God determines whether a particular subjective response is appropriate. However, in searching for the properly personal or intuitive dimension of religious life, some theistic existentialists denigrate the facticity of history and the status of doctrine. They look instead for the "existential meaning" or "personal truth" behind historical narrative and doctrinal statements.

Philosophical Analysis: Logic and Linguistics

Although analytic philosophy rejects the aims of systematic philosophy, it does not simply replace traditional views of reality, knowledge and value with new and different ones. Philosophical analysis is not interested in making metaphysical, epistemological or axiological statements. Instead it is concerned with clarification of the concepts and language we employ in doing philosophy. This shift in orientation means that we cannot discuss analytic philosophy in terms of its answers to the traditional questions of philosophy.

In spite of vigorous disagreements among analysts, their rallying point is the conviction that philosophy must clarify the ways we use language. They view some philosophical problems as aggravated by misleading forms of discourse. Analysis has become a dominant way of engaging in philosophical activity, particularly in the United States and Great Britain.

The analytic movement can be roughly divided into two broad schools of thought: one which seeks better understanding of ordinary language and one which attempts to construct an ideal language. Many analysts took Ludwig Wittgenstein's *Tractatus Logico-Philosophicus* to express an ideal language project:

Philosophy is aimed at the logical clarification of thoughts.

Philosophy is not a body of doctrine but an activity.

A philosophical work consists essentially of elucidations.

Philosophy does not result in "philosophical propositions," but rather in the clarification of propositions.

Without philosophy thoughts are, as it were, cloudy and indistinct: its task is to make them clear and to give them sharp boundaries.[24]

These lines, written at the beginning of Wittgenstein's career, were commonly cited as disdaining the ambiguity of ordinary language.

The search for an ideal language spawned logical positivism, a very influential movement. With roots in the empiricism of John Locke and David Hume, positivism sought the meaning of all language through empirical verifiability. Particularly interested in devising an inclusive logical system for all sciences, positivists declared that all statements which could not be tested by scientific criteria are meaningless.[25] The meaningfulness of the propositions of metaphysics, theology and ethics was immediately thrown into question. Having had its heyday in the earlier portions of this century, logical positivism has now been supplanted by the ordinary language approach.

Interestingly, ordinary language analysis, which superseded positivism, was also inspired by Wittgenstein. His later writings, especially the *Philosophical Investigations,* inspired much activity among ordinary language philosophers. Philosophers—Peter Strawson, John Austin, John Wisdom and others—believe that common language is adequate for human purposes; we simply need to understand its functioning better. Ordinary language philosophers try to elucidate the concepts and beliefs which language embodies. A hallmark of this phase of analytic philosophy is its new openness to the meaningfulness of statements which do not conform to the empirical criteria of science proposed by the positivists. But current analysts still believe that philosophical problems are rooted in linguistic confusions.[26]

Philosophical Analysis and the Educative Process

The relation of analytic philosophy to education is quite different from the relationship of the various "systems" of philosophy to the educational endeavor. Traditional philosophical positions typically provide general concepts of reality, knowledge and value, and then draw their implications for education. Analyst R. S. Peters states that the historical function of philosophical systems is "the formulation of high-level directives which would guide educational practice and shape the organization of schools."[27]

Most analytic philosophers hold that the current task of philosophy is not to assert philosophical premises and then draw educational prescriptions from them. Instead philosophy should clarify the ways we think and speak about educational matters. As Peters indicates, the job of the analytic philosopher is to position our basic concepts and commitments "under the analytic guillotine."[28] He means that analysis should dissect our educational concepts and terms with the goal of elucidating their meaning and use.

The aim of clarity leads analytic educational philosophers to try to adopt a neutral stance. Arnold Levison writes:

Analytic philosophy can help analyze and clarify language, provide models of theory, state criteria for meaning and verification, and in general, help unsnarl the logical and linguistic tangles in pedagogical knowledge.[29]

Since analytic philosophers do not prescribe educational goals or norms, we cannot discuss their positions on such issues as curriculum structure and pedagogy, as with previous philosophical approaches.

One example of the analytic approach to education would be the clarification of the experimentalist dictum "Teachers should provide real life experiences for their students." This rule is intended to discourage too much formal, and supposedly artificial, academic exercise. The analytic philosopher could point out that the term "real life" is a descriptive term which refers to all of the activities of human beings. Grammar is an activity of human beings. Therefore, why should conjugating verbs be ruled out of the original prescription—something which the experimentalist wants to do?[30] Other items for analysis include "good life," "learning," "liberal education," "culture," "curriculum" and so on.

William Frankena goes further than Peters and many other analysts. He claims that analytic philosophy should not only explicate the meanings of educational terms, but map the logic of educational philosophy as a whole region of discourse. This useful mapping activity allows us to navigate within a subject successfully. Frankena believes that such a procedure can help us understand normative philosophies of education and can enable us to build our own philosophy of education.[31]

"Education," Frankena maintains, "is the process by which society makes of its members what it is desirable that they should become . . . either in general or insofar as this may be carried on by what are called 'schools.' "[32] The main task of a normative philosophy of education, he thinks, is to list and define a set of dispositions to be fostered by parents and teachers. Frankena offers a model of how this list fits into an overall philosophy of education.[33]

Frankena's model (diagrammed on the next page) identifies the types of sentences in a philosophy of education and the ways they are related to each other. Frankena believes that his model helps us understand the elements and structure of a normative philosophy of education.

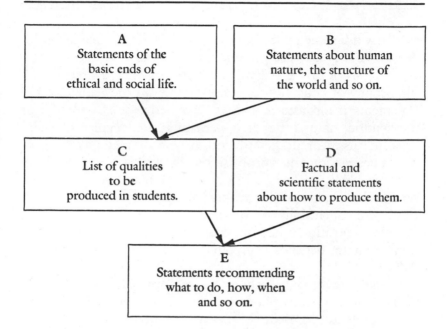

If providing a list of desirable traits is central to a normative philosophy of education, then that list is both a conclusion from higher-level commitments and a premise for drawing more specific directions for education. On the one hand, a complete philosophy of education provides a line of thought showing that the specified dispositions (C) are indeed desirable. Such a rationale will draw from our most basic normative judgments about life (A) and our overall world view and general knowledge (B). On the other hand, the list of qualities (C), together with certain factual information about how dispositions are produced (D), function as grounds for making more specific recommendations about how and when to produce them (E). This list of concrete recommendations pertains to curriculum, pedagogy and so on.

Obviously, a total normative philosophy of education has a more theoretical side (ABC pattern) and a more practical side (CDE pattern). Frankena explains that a philosophy of education may use some premises from box B to draw conclusions in box D. And it may use premises from boxes A and B to draw conclusions in box E.[34] Frankena notes that the character of a philosophy of education depends heavily on the nature of the statements it includes in B and D. Whether it is scientific or unscientific, naturalistic or supernaturalistic, secular or religious, idealistic or pragmatic, positivistic or metaphysical, depends entirely on what propositions it employs in B and D in order to reach conclusions in C and E. Frankena also elaborates on the significance of the propositions affirmed in A, since no normative conclusions can be drawn in C and E without them. Whether a position is hedonistic or nonhedonistic, utilitarian or nonutilitarian, depends completely on the premises asserted in A.[35]

Frankena says that his scheme can be applied to the educational thought of various philosophers (for instance, Plato, Rousseau, Whitehead, Dewey, Maritain), but briefly discusses Aristotle to illustrate his model. He indicates that a portion of Aristotle's work on education exhibits the ABC pattern. Aristotle's statement that the good life is a happy one consisting of intrinsically excellent activities (such as contemplation) belongs to box A. Furthermore, Aristotle's belief that if we are to achieve the good life, we must cultivate certain dispositions (for example, moderation, practical wisdom and a knowledge of mathematics, physics and philosophy) belongs to box B. Aristotle's conclusion that we ought to cultivate such dispositions belongs to box C. Aristotle then used this conclusion, conjoined with certain other philosophical beliefs in box B and empirical observations in box D, to generate definite recommendations about the most effective methods for cultivating desired dispositions (such as habit formation) in box E.[36]

Evaluating Philosophical Analysis

Analytic procedures can improve educational philosophy by

clarifying key terms and concepts, pointing out implications of philosophical statements, and examining the structure of educational theories. Analytic philosophers differ over the exact proportion of analytic procedures to more substantive theorizing. For Peters, philosophy of education is exclusively analytic. Frankena, however, believes that philosophy of education should include both analytic and normative aspects. For him, analysis can hone the logic and detail of our thinking, and the synoptic and normative approach can create a comprehensive vision of education.[37]

Analytic philosophers portray themselves as having metaphysically and morally neutral positions, but almost inevitably operate on the basis of certain tacit philosophical assumptions. Historically, some analysts have held assumptions very compatible with materialism and empiricism, and hence are open to the same criticisms as those positions. Peters is a case in point. He would restrict the premises to be used in box B of Frankena's model to empirical or scientific ones.

Narrowly empirical assumptions cause peculiar trouble when analytic philosophers examine the linguistic and conceptual structures of Christianity. Obviously, materialistic and positivistic assumptions influence how analytic methods are applied to language and thought about God, morality and so on. Logical positivists, for example, concluded that propositions about nonempirical realities are meaningless. The same assumptions which damage the meaning of theological claims are also devastating to Christian educational statements. Talk of the inherent worth of students as persons and a transcendent purpose to life which education must recognize would be ruled out.

Not all analytic philosophers hold positivistic assumptions. While many analytic thinkers are positivists, some are idealists and a growing number are theists. There is no necessary link between a single philosophical position and analytic methods. Analysis should not be impugned simply because many of its adherents have been positivists. It is advisable to investigate rigorously the linguistic and conceptual features of philosophical positions or even those of the Christian faith. The moral is not to allow the presuppositions of an analysis to distort its findings.[38] With due care, analysis can be an ally in building a general Christian world view and philosophy of education in particular.

4

Toward a
Christian Perspective
on Education

*A*fter examining the educational implications of various philosophical positions, we must explore the educational implications of a Christian world view. So far we have seen the relation of Christianity to educational thinking only by way of commentary on other philosophies. Following the organization of previous chapters, we will sketch a Christian world view by addressing the main questions of reality, knowledge and value. Then we will analyze their impact on curriculum structure, methods of teaching and learning, and value education.

Seventeen centuries ago the church father Tertullian asked the question: "What, indeed, has Athens to do with Jerusalem? What concord is there between the Academy and the Church?"[1] Of course, what Tertullian was asking is: What is the relationship between reason and the pursuit of worldly knowledge, on the one hand, and faith and the revelation of God, on the other?

Tertullian's own answer is implied in a rhetorical way in the question itself. He held not only that Christian revelation is self-sufficient, but that there is tension or conflict between the spiritual mission of the church and the intellectual role of the academy. This position is clearly a minority one in the history of Christian thought.

The majority of Christian thinkers have declared an important and intimate relationship between the life of the intellect and the life of faith.[2] They hold that a Christian perspective readily embraces education. This comprehensive world view combines fundamental themes from historic Christian theology with the best insights from philosophy. The result is a unique vision of God, reality, humanity, history, culture, knowledge, morality and value—a vision which endorses the educational enterprise in distinctive ways. Much of what we find in this vision will resonate with the Neo-Thomistic position but will be supplemented by contributions from the broader Christian community.

Christianity and Metaphysics

If metaphysics is the central concern of a world view, then creational metaphysics is central to a Christian world view. Christian orthodoxy accepts two broad categories of existence: God, the Creator, and the world, his creation. Beyond these two realities there is nothing else. When we recite the Apostle's Creed ("I believe in God the Father Almighty, Maker of heaven and earth . . ."), we affirm this truth.

Historic Christian thought holds that the infinite and sovereign God, who alone is eternal and self-sufficient, freely chose to create everything that is out of absolutely nothing. Penetrating insights into the nature of our world and the meaning of the human endeavor can be unfolded from this point.

Daniel O'Connor and Francis Oakley claim that the doctrine of creation is completely radical. It is not only the central motif in any exposition of a Christian world view, but is also a conception of reality utterly distinct from that of competing religions and philosophies:

> The idea of creation brings in its wake a whole chain of implications. Not that they were all perceived at once. Centuries were required before some of them—for example, those affecting conceptions of personality or the nature of the political life—were clearly understood.[3]

O'Connor and Oakley proceed to trace the special implications of the Judeo-Christian concept of creation.

It is not so much the idea of a beginning which makes the doctrine of creation unique. The distinctiveness of the biblical doctrine of creation is its stress on the fact that all beings are totally dependent on a transcendent, personal source. In contrast to other cosmologies, the biblical account does not hold that the world is identical with God (as does Hindu pantheism) or an emanation from his being (as in Neo-Platonism). Nor is the world the product of a struggle between dualistic entities, such as God and Evil (as in ancient Babylonian religion) or a combination of good and evil elements (as in Platonism). The world is a creature of a sovereign and loving God, dependent on his will for its source and sustenance.

Among the immediate implications of the doctrine of creation are the notion of meaningful history and the idea of a moral dimension of reality. A proper view of creation understands history as the arena in which human beings act. Their plans and activities are not determined by an arbitrary deity or by the stuff out of which they are made. God interacts with human choices, but protects their significance. After all, he made us by fiat and endowed us with many finite powers similar to his own infinite powers: reason, emotion and will. Hence our individual and collective destinies are truly our own.

In contrast to many rival theologies and philosophies, the biblical picture of creation places moral responsibility squarely on the shoulders of human beings. People are independent moral beings and not part of some divine or primordial substance. Thus it is possible for their choices to be independent and free. And since the world is created and sustained by a transcendent personal being, we are obliged to conform to the moral structures he has established. The Old Testament picture of a God of covenantal relations rests on the fundamental perception that God is moral and that our transactions with him and with our fellows must be premised on moral grounds.[4]

Certain implications of the doctrine of creation bear more directly on the philosophy of education. First, it follows from the doctrine that the created world—the one we touch and see—is real. Second, it follows that nature is intelligible. Since nature is a creature of a supremely creative mind, it is open to rational investigation by finite minds. Third, the idea of creation implies that the whole created world is good. Coming without flaw from the creative activity of a perfect being, this world has great worth. In spite of the fact that sin has alienated the creation from its Creator, the basic value of the creation remains intact. The Christian conception of reality, then, contradicts all views which hold the world to be illusory, unintelligible or evil.

Against the backdrop of the general concept of creation, a biblical anthropology can be developed. The starting place for a proper view of humanity is that point of contact we have with all of nature: creatureliness. Human beings are finite, fallible and perishable—characteristics which do not differentiate them from the nonhuman creation. Like all things, persons are created beings, dependent for their existence on a source higher than nature. Yet somehow present within the elements of our creaturehood is the image of God *(imago Dei)*, which distinguishes humans from nonhuman creatures. Our personhood is a reflection of the nature of a transcendent God.

In this context, personhood must be defined in that rich and full sense which involves the many powers of reason, the vistas of emotion and feeling, and the ability to choose. In a sense, a person is a miniature creator, capable of understanding and doing things within a limited sphere of existence which somehow parallel what the omnipotent deity can accomplish. The concept of personhood in the image of God can be further extended to include the idea of a singular center of consciousness which has a special privacy or interiority to itself, but which needs to find fulfillment in relationship with others. Additional ramifications of the concept include insights into the nature of sexuality, the meaning of work and vocation, the role of play and so forth.[5] Certainly, further elaboration of a biblical anthropology would involve a Christological point of reference. The key to reality, and the key to human reality in particular, is Jesus Christ.[6]

Christianity and Epistemology

The fact that God has made persons to be creatures who form beliefs and seek knowledge ushers us right to the threshold of epistemology. To be sure, God's knowledge is total, perfect and impeccable while ours is partial, defective and fallible. Yet bearing the image of God, we are able to think, judge and know in some ways which reflect God's thoughts, judgments and knowledge. A theistic world view does not guarantee that our efforts to attain knowledge will be free from error, but assures us that we have been endowed with the ability to gain some reliable knowledge about reality.

A complete Christian view of knowledge recognizes that reality is complex and that each of its domains must be known on its own terms. There is no single way to discover all the different truths there are. We must discover empirical truths through observation and experiment, historical truths through records and artifacts, logical and mathematical truths by abstract reasoning, and so forth. Christians have no shortcuts for acquiring truths in these areas, but share the same basic noetic capabilities as other humans.

What Christians can have is a world view which gives truth

an appropriate residence. Christian theism affirms that the world is real and that there can be genuine knowledge of it. Since there is such a thing as truth, one of the deepest longings of our being can be satisfied. A Christian epistemological orientation would dismiss at the outset any theory of knowledge which distorts the kinds of knowledge available in a theistic universe. For example, extreme empiricism, which holds that knowledge comes exclusively through the senses, is rejected. But the fact that some knowledge comes through sense perception is a point which a Christian epistemology would grant.

Moreover, there is a Christological center for knowledge. Jesus Christ is said to be "the word of God," "the wisdom of God," "the one in whom all of the knowledge of God rests." This suggests that the very heart of reality is rational, and that all other knowledge takes on proper perspective through relationship to Christ. Thus knowledge has a center and a ground.

Christianity and Axiology

Christian theism provides a theory of value which fits consistently with the foregoing theories of reality and knowledge. Christian ethics rests on the conviction that the Creator of reality is completely moral and that his creation exhibits a moral structure. At the outset, the Judeo-Christian world view denies all positions which take fundamental moral principles to be either meaningless (as in varieties of emotivism and subjectivism) or relative (for instance, situationism). Moral principles are meaningful and unchanging because they reflect absolute moral realities.

None of this is to deny the fact that persons and cultures sometimes differ in their formulations of fundamental moral principles or apply them in different ways. The very fact that we do communicate on moral issues—disagreeing, persuading one another and reaching decisions—indicates that there is cognitive content to moral judgments. The fact that most if not all societies agree on the most basic values (love, justice, benevolence and so forth) demonstrates that there is a common moral perception among people, in spite of the fact that they do not always share less essential preferences.[7]

In addition to rejecting moral theories which are subjectivistic or relativistic, a Christian world view rejects the basic tenets of both ethical egoism and utilitarianism. While we will not attempt to unearth all of the problems of such ethical theories, we must note one common flaw which is crucial: they countenance no actions, or kinds of action, as being inherently good or evil. Ethical egoism recommends that whatever advances the interests of the individual be morally acceptable. Utilitarianism requires whatever action furthers the interests of society. Under certain conditions, egoism and utilitarianism would even endorse actions which our common moral experience woud take to be evil.

The world view of Christian theism offers a concept of intrinsic goodness, that is, goodness which does not depend on some extrinsic factor. While other ethical theories are bankrupt at this point, creational metaphysics, with its premium on personhood, provides an important insight into the ontological basis of values.[8] The concept of persons being made in the image of God provides the ontological ground for ethics. Because humans are the kind of creatures they are—rational, moral, social beings— certain moral considerations are due them. Keith Yandell explains that the ontological structure of personhood accords it "inherent value" which cannot be outweighed by the moral consideration of anything which is nonpersonal.[9] In contemporary parlance, this conception of ethics is *deontological.*

Christian theism also provides the framework for a theory of nonmoral and aesthetic values. The biblical tradition affirms that the whole universe is filled with the glory of God, an affirmation which easily translates into the truth that the world is charged with value. A host of nonmoral goods or values are available in our world: friendship, knowledge, pleasure, love, loyalty and others. Christianity understands these goods as being gracious gifts of God, manifestations of his love in creation.

Although thoughtful Christians may differ on the controversial issue of beauty, some general insights can be developed in harmony with the preceding remarks on metaphysics and epistemology. Just as reality is not illusory and truth is not completely subjective, beauty is not merely a private preference. Beauty in an object is a kind of excellence or perfection. Elements of beauty might include unity, proportion and clarity.[10] The perception of beauty in this sense generally must be cultivated and will naturally be keener in those who are well instructed. Judgments of beauty conceived in this way have an objective reference, although there can still be disagreement about the standards of beauty or about what specimens (whether natural or humanly made) are beautiful.

The counterpart to the objective beauty which exists in the world is the subjective response of persons. Certain things please individuals in various ways. We often talk about objects as being beautiful, not so much because they have an intrinsically excellent nature, but because we have certain emotional reactions to them. Claims that things we enjoy are beautiful are essentially expressions of taste. Both kinds of human appreciation of beauty are legitimate. Subjective beauty, within the sphere of taste, has a very affective character, whereas objective beauty involves certain cognitive functions as well. God has created persons to seek beauty and its appropriate pleasures. And the beauty and pleasure we find are actually hints of God in the created order, glimpses of his perfection and grace.

Talk of the goods found in creation inevitably raises the age-old problem of evil and suffering. The classic Christian explanation revolves around the concept of our divinely created freedom which made possible the Fall. The subsequent alienation from God has meant that various sorts of creaturely goods are sometimes perverted. Christianity envisions a particular program for God's redemption of humanity and the rest of creation, a program presently in progress and moving toward a future culmination.[11]

A Christian Justification of Education

Neither the Bible nor a general Christian view of life contains an explicit philosophy of education. However, a Christian world view provides certain implications for education. These implications apply to education conducted within both the public and private domains, and to education at all levels. As with previous perspectives, a Christian world view affects curriculum structure, teaching and learning styles, and the development of character and taste.

The starting place for a Christian philosophy of education is the innate human tendency to seek understanding. This divinely created tendency finds sophisticated corporate expression in formal education. Formal education represents a sustained effort to record, systematize and transmit the knowledge and culture which we have attained. From a biblical point of view, the school is not merely an outgrowth of a natural tendency in humankind, but is mandated in God's command for Adam to "take dominion" over the created order. "Taking dominion" ultimately implies rational supervision and control—and education is one logical extension of this idea. In principle, then, the school can be interpreted as a divinely ordained, human institution.

Interestingly, many theologies of education—particularly Protestant ones—have failed to see education in this light. Many religious theories of education proclaim that the divinely ordained, human institutions are exactly three in number: the family, the church and the state. Depending on which theology of education we read, then, education becomes a derivative of one or the other of the three fundamental institutions. But such views seem to depend either on an overly literalistic reading of Genesis or an inadequate concept of education. In terms of the very nature of humanity no good argument seems possible for accepting the family, church and state, but rejecting the school, as divinely ordained institutions. Of course, although logically distinct from the other institutions, formal education historically grew out of them. And the other three institutions remain committed to various kinds of education and training.[12]

While we may affirm a status and dignity for formal education which is uniquely its own, it would be a mistake to assume that the proper domain of education is "secular" or "worldly" knowledge, whereas the domain of the church is "sacred" or "spiritual" knowledge. Christian theism collapses the misleading sacred-secular distinction altogether.[13] God is one; he is a unity. All truth stems from him and is known by him. Since all truth is God's, wherever it may be found, there is no basis for insisting that only "religious knowledge" has spiritual significance. Neither is there basis for saying that a religious vocation is of greater value than any other. When done for the glory of God, the most mundane tasks—such as political involvement, full-time home-making, business undertakings and disciplined study—have eternal worth. In a very real sense, therefore, legitimate involvement in creation, conducted in light of the truth we know, is sacred.

Christianity and the Curriculum
In light of the high status of education within a Christian world view, how can we outline an educational philosophy? In a well-formed philosophy of education, metaphysics virtually determines curriculum structure: the subjects and sequence of studies should reflect the various areas of reality which are recognized. A further metaphysical consideration which influences curriculum regards the nature of humanity and how it can be developed by formal schooling. Christian theism advances the principle that each person should be aided to develop his or her God-given potential to the fullest.

The realistic metaphysics of Christian theism advanced here

holds that a human being is a unity of rational, emotional, moral and practical dimensions. Limiting our discussion to the rational and practical aspects of personhood, what can be said about the shape of the curriculum? Although we must not dichotomize these two aspects of personhood, it is reasonable to think that, to some extent, two different sorts of study will aid the development of these dual aspects. The point of curriculum design, then, is to clarify what sort of development is desired and how it should be accomplished.

It could be argued that the rational part of a human being, which itself does not change, should be nourished on lasting truths and great ideas which are relatively unchanging. These themes will mainly be about humanity itself, our moral quest and the meaning of our place in the universe. Even though people and cultures down through the centuries have held differing views on these subjects, studying these ideas provides the opportunity for each person and each generation to think through the fundamental issues. Much insight is available to those who try to understand the reasons for disagreement among views and who perceive their underlying agreement.

While a Christian position accords dignity to the practical part of personhood (an aspect which may involve manual labor or other activities of creaturely survival), purely practical involvement is limited in its ability to help us gain a larger understanding of life. That is why nourishing students on the major themes and great ideas of humankind helps them transcend the spatiotemporal boundaries inherent in most of practical life. It enables them to think not simply in terms of their immediate surroundings or needs, but in terms of the global situation in which humanity finds itself. It sensitizes them to moral obligations, religious aspirations and the recurring problems of the race. It brings a more complete perspective to bear on practical decision and action. When speaking of what this kind of education had done for him, Aristotle stated that it had allowed him to do freely what most persons do as slaves. In other words, broad understanding and mental freedom give direction to practical action.

An actual curriculum featuring the enduring themes about God, humanity and the world would include such subjects as the natural sciences, the social and human sciences, mathematics, history, literature and philosophy. Components of a curriculum aimed at practical training are a somewhat different matter, as the precise content and form of training depends on the desirable skills in an ever-changing job market. In choosing a curriculum which best meets the needs of the whole person, it is extremely important for educators to be clear about what kinds of realities they seek to feature and what kinds of human potentials they want to develop.

The effect of metaphysics on the curriculum pertains to all levels of schooling, from elementary through college. The version of Christian theism espoused here suggests that reality has a determinate structure created by God. Knowledge of reality therefore has a structure. Education, then, imparts knowledge of the structure of reality. However, the curriculum must adjust the way knowledge is presented to the developmental stage of the learner. Earlier stages of schooling must provide the basic skills, techniques and concepts for acquiring later, more mature forms of knowledge.

Jerome Bruner suggests that a sound curriculum would be designed in a "spiral." As students progress and move from one instructional level to another, "a curriculum . . . should revisit . . . basic ideas repeatedly, building upon them until the student has grasped the full formal apparatus that goes with them."[14] The preparatory function of early schooling also includes positive emotional support, initial socialization, the beginnings of character development, physical hygiene and coordination, and the capabilities to navigate in the world.

Further exploration of the philosophical base of the curriculum is needed. But the point here is that Christian theism supports conforming the curriculum to the structure of reality and the nature of humanity. It provides a sound metaphysical interpretation of the many facets of human beings and their temporal development. A total Christian view does not isolate one aspect of humanity from the others; it conceives of our nature as a composite unity. A Christian view also correctly conceives of how education enables us to fulfill certain dimensions of our humanity. While recognizing that the school should help develop the various capacities of childhood and adolescence, a Christian position urges that these capacities must become ever more mature. Ultimately, it is not the world of the child, but the real world—of serious decision, human conflict, work and leisure, success and failure, triumph and tragedy—for which the process of education is to prepare the student. It would be a crime against youth if we allowed education to foster, even for a moment, the delusion that the world is just for them or that reality conforms to their relatively immature ways of thinking about it. In a world which virtually worships youth, this insight may become increasingly important.

Christianity, Teaching and Learning

Modes of teaching and learning are influenced by epistemological commitments. For a Christian theist, teaching and learning must be built on the confidence that we can know reality, that truth about the world is accessible to our investigations. The principle of commitment to truth, whether anyone's idiosyncratic interests are served by it or not, must be the cardinal presupposition of intellectual activity.[15] At the outset, commitment to truth avoids the underlying skepticism of our age. The pervasive epistemic skepticism which surfaces in our schools, particularly high schools and colleges, is only one of the many forms which skepticism takes. Students eventually get the message that one cannot know the answers to life's most important questions.

In an environment which has no way of determining the answers to basic human questions, the whole academic enterprise becomes downgraded. Two characteristics of our educational milieu are relativism and radical freedom. Relativism treats all of life's major options as if they were of equal value, and radical freedom recommends that, in the absence of any way to tell which option is correct, each person's opinion simply be accepted as true. In such an environment the pragmatic and practical courses of study generally persist unaffected. However, those studies which deal with large issues—the destiny of humanity, the nature of ultimate reality and the grounds of moral obligation—become regarded as fantasy or, at best, interesting word games which people play.

An educational enterprise that is grounded in the mind's ability to know the truth is prepared to benefit from the best research on how knowledge is acquired and transferred. We must be careful, however, in drawing recommendatory conclusions from purely factual research. We should not assume that currently accepted modes of teaching and learning can go without question. For example, studies by Chickering and others suggest that the bulk of modern college students are oriented to learn from concrete, empirical experience.[16] Nevertheless it does not automatically follow that this is the only way we should teach them. Perhaps these students are deficient and need to find out how to learn at an abstract, cognitive level. But research alone will not uncover this need. The Christian theist must appeal to a more adequate epistemology which places a premium on the refined powers of intellect. Hence, epistemology should interact with the available research in order to develop a proper theory of teaching and learning styles.[17]

We are not without some collective wisdom on the issue of teaching and learning styles. Drawing from historical educational experience, Mortimer Adler proposes that there are three basic modes of teaching and learning, which correspond exactly to three basic ways in which the mind can be improved: (1) the acquisition of organized knowledge; (2) the development of intellectual skills; and (3) the enlargement of understanding, insight and appreciation.[18] The ideal is that the three main types of educational processes will interact in all courses and at all levels of schooling.

It is typically recommended that the most fundamental branches of organized knowledge (language, literature, mathematics, history, social studies and the natural sciences) be taught through the use of didactic methods and textbooks. Much of this education will almost necessarily be rote, but not exclusively so. The mental preparation of students in these areas of knowledge can begin in attractive ways in the early grades and build continuity as the students progress.

The very backbone of education is the development of basic skills: reading, writing, speaking, listening, observing, measuring, estimating and calculating. Since this type of knowledge is "knowledge how to do" rather than "knowledge about," it can most effectively be gained by performance, practice and drill. To impart this kind of learning, the teacher must be like an athletic coach, guiding students in the doing of certain things, correcting faulty performances and eventually helping them to achieve a measure of proficiency.

The enlargement of the understanding and appreciation rests on but transcends basic knowledge and skills. Its goal is to bring ideas to birth in the students' minds, improve critical judgment, tutor moral sentiments, stimulate enjoyment and admiration of beauty, enhance the imagination and increase tolerance. The materials for such teaching, according to Adler, are the great works of civilization and culture: the great books, pieces of art and documents which treat the important issues of human life. The pedagogical approach to this consummate phase of education is, as it should be, the Socratic method. The interrogative or discussion format is geared to improve both synthetic and analytic powers and to awaken the creative and inquisitive capacities of the students.

Christianity and Value Education

The axiological commitments of Christian theism shape our thinking about ethical and aesthetic education. For the Christian, objects and actions in the universe have value, both moral and nonmoral. From this point, a general sketch of value education can be drawn.

The impetus for moral education is the fact that God is holy and that he created humans as moral beings capable of reflecting that holiness to some degree. We are moral agents, able to know and do what is right. The task of moral education, then, is to help youth realize this aspect of their human nature. A comprehensive approach anchors the objectives of moral education in a theory of what it means to be a moral agent. Christian theism takes a moral agent, at the very least, to be a person who makes moral judgments and performs morally significant actions. Correspondingly, the taxonomy of moral education contains at least two domains, the cognitive and the behavioral. In this context, the cognitive domain pertains to our consciousness of moral considerations and our ability to make moral evaluations. The behavioral domain relates to our tendencies to act in moral ways, to put our ethical knowledge into practice.

The process of moral education, therefore, will be concerned with determining the proper sources of moral knowledge and the best means for conveying it to children and youth. Christian theism takes the two major sources of moral knowledge to be the common moral experience of the human race, on the one hand, and the precepts and principles of the Old and New Testaments, on the other. The former source is available to all persons insofar as they are rational and moral creatures; it is part of God's general revelation.[19] The latter source, God's special revelation, clarifies and intensifies the nature of our moral obligations and shows that the whole moral enterprise is rooted in a morally perfect Creator. Properly interpreted, the legitimate sources of moral knowledge concur in the moral obligations they deliver. We have moral responsibilities to deity, to ourselves, to our fellow human beings and to nature. Both sources of moral knowledge also indicate that something is unmistakably wrong in the moral endeavor, a condition which the Bible identifies as sin.

The Judeo-Christian Scriptures contain little by way of specific directives for moral education. These we must glean from the most reasonable theories, the best empirical research and common sense—all supply insight into our creaturely nature. A complete Christian view of moral education, however, does not focus exclusively on the natural channels of moral education and ignore God's grace for moral living. While taking seriously the fact that there are natural means of developing moral capabilities, a Christian view of moral education heralds the concept of God's grace which completes and uplifts nature.

A complete Christian world view affirms that aesthetic education is an important part of a student's value education. Works of art are mirrors of the human condition and provide a significant avenue of understanding how different artists, cultures and epochs have understood God, humanity and the world. Helpful recommendations for aesthetic education include discussing fine works of art (whether poetry or fiction, drama or dance, painting or sculpture) both from the standpoint of their underlying message and their specific art form.

Generally, great works of art need additional treatment in order to be appreciated aesthetically, to be enjoyed and admired for their inherent excellence. They need to be experienced in a way appropriate to their nature as art. Art invites participation: great music needs to be played; great drama needs to be performed; and great painting needs to be viewed at length. Students should not only participate in the great and classic works of art, but also attempt to create art of their very own. Every student, at every grade level, needs this kind of pleasurable experience.

The ultimate goal of aesthetic education is to enable students to become more self-conscious and discriminating in what they enjoy as well as to improve their sensitivity to and judgment about what is admirable. The hope is that this kind of education ultimately enhances all of life. It may be that those who have had glimpses of beauty will be able to improve a world in which there is increasing tension and pressure.

5

Issues in
Educational Theory

*C*omplexities abound in educational circles today. America has now moved past the explosive problem of racial desegregation and the controversy over progressivism. Now different issues are gaining increased attention: the teaching of creation and evolution, tax credits for private tuition, sex education and others. In Britain, peace studies and women's studies are gaining importance. A sound educational philosophy should provide guidance for thinking about these and other subjects.

Some contemporary issues are theoretical, relating to how we understand various aspects of education in light of basic philosophical assumptions. Other issues are more practical, pertaining to how we conduct the business of education in view of current social conditions. The present chapter discusses several issues which can be roughly classified as theoretical: liberal learning and general education, the integration of faith and learning, education in morals and values, pedagogy and the educational enterprise. The following chapter discusses certain issues which are more practical: liberal education and vocational training, public and private education, academic rights and freedoms, teaching and indoctrination. All issues are treated in terms of the Christian orientation toward education already developed.

Liberal Learning and General Education

In curricular discussions, liberal education is often equated with general education. General education is usually arranged in a basic "core" of courses which students are required to take. From elementary through high school, the core typically features basic skills and knowledge. Courses in a college general curriculum offer even more abstract and sophisticated knowledge which is viewed as essential. However, the relationship of a general education to a liberal one needs careful analysis.

The connection of a general education to liberal learning is that of means to end. Liberal learning (as distinct from vocational training) is the goal; it prizes mental freedom and responsibility, and a tolerant and humane spirit. A broad course of studies (as distinct from a specialized or professional one) has long been a favored means of reaching that goal. Although this means-end relationship should be clarified in curricular deliberations for all grades, it needs vigorous discussion in higher education.

Interestingly, a liberal education is not necessarily a purely general one, since a free and critical mind *could* be developed by the study of just one or a few particular disciplines. Indeed, the subjects originally included in a liberal arts curriculum were relatively small in number. In the Middle Ages, the trivium (grammar, logic and rhetoric) and the quadrivium (arithmetic, geometry, astronomy and music) constituted the liberal arts and helped produce very good minds.[1]

So students might develop the ability to think critically within the methodology of a certain few disciplines and thereby gain a habit of thought which will stand them in good stead in a variety of situations. Conversely, a general education is not necessarily a liberal one, since an uncritical and slavish mind *might* be produced through the study of many and varied subjects. For example, a student might memorize a great deal of facts about many academic areas, credulously believe each textbook and each teacher in turn, and end up rather small-minded and role-bound.

There are, of course, impressive reasons to think that general learning is a good basis for a liberal education. But a general education is neither a necessary nor a sufficient condition for a liberal education. Hence, we must return to our philosophical foundations in order to understand what key factors enable a general education to be liberating. Actually, there are two distinct conceptions of why general studies should compose a liberal curriculum, each based on a different desired outcome. Richard Burke entitles these the Platonic and the Protagorean conceptions of general education.[2]

In the *Republic*, Plato proposed that all knowledge claims be examined for objective truth. He taught that "dialectic"—the art of dialoging and reasoning through the interplay of ideas—was essential in order to get at what is true. Plato believed that human thought and decision are free only as they conform to truth about reality. Mental and moral freedom were the goals of the general education which he offered. The other conception of general education, named after Protagoras, the ancient Sophist, is "rhetorical" rather than "dialectical." The Protagorean rationale for a general education is that students need wide acquaintance with different ideas and opinions in order to communicate with others in society and persuade them to their own view. It is not essential to this rhetorical theory of general education that there be some way of ascertaining which view is correct or true. Hence, a virtual skepticism is accepted toward truth and the means of determining it. Freedom on this view pertains not to the rational control of one's impulses in light of truth and duty, but to the ability to hold one's own in human commerce.

There is one striking difference between these two conceptions of general education. The dialectical approach holds that there are certain themes and truths which every student should study, whereas the rhetorical one holds that it does not matter much what students study as long as it relates to current society. A general education, for the dialectical program, means that there should be a broad base in knowledge essential to our humanity, in learning which pertains to the large, perennial issues of human thought and action. The student should be brought to consider certain pervasive concerns about the nature of the universe, the meaning of life and our common duty—as a prelude to working out his or her own frame of reference.

The Platonic or dialectical model dominated education for centuries. Most of the Hellenic and Roman schools followed it in establishing the trivium and quadrivium as the standard of education. In medieval Europe the study of Holy Scripture was incorporated into educational patterns and the trivium and quadrivium were reinterpreted to coincide with its teaching. From the Renaissance to the nineteenth century, the content of education shifted from theology to the humanities: the philosophy, literature, history and art of ancient Greece and Rome. In contemporary times, the content of a liberal education in this tradition has been changed somewhat to include various subjects which the educated person must know something about: world history, scientific interpretations of the universe, theories of the social sciences, great literature and philosophy. The attempt has not been to be excessively broad, but to include the kinds of learning which foster rational and moral control of human affairs and enlightened understanding of the human condition.[3]

On the rhetorical scheme, a general education means that there should be broad exposure to as many different viewpoints as possible, a learning which reflects the varied opinions extant in the modern world. This view denies that it is important for students to know about anything in particular and considers dogmatic the claim that certain kinds of knowledge are more worthwhile or more humanizing than others—the intellectual tyranny of some subjects over others. In recent decades, during which American universities have seemed to opt for this model, we have seen course offerings for a "liberal" education include transcendental meditation as well as psychology, astrology as well as astronomy, Fortran as well as foreign language, gay history as well as world civilization. While these examples are a bit extreme, they nonetheless expose the bankruptcy of the rhetorical approach to education and suggest its inability to produce a properly liberated intelligence.

One main cause of such curricular deficiencies is the loss of a coherent understanding of what liberal learning really is. When liberal learning is mistakenly equated with a general selection of courses, then there is no basis for holding that some courses are more important to our humanity than others and thus should be required of all seeking a degree. Of course, there are good reasons for introducing courses, say, in Eastern religions or feminist studies. Certainly, a liberally educated person must be willing to learn from a variety of perspectives and be aware of their critiques of traditional Western views. The point is that all studies should be evaluated in terms of their promotion of the goal of liberal education.

Administrators and faculty who arrange their general curriculum by requiring "a little of each subject" or letting students "pick a course from each group" are forfeiting the high, Platonic conception of liberal learning and the precise kind of general education it demands. The lower, Protagorean conception typically dominates when there is no guiding philosophical consensus about what courses constitute a truly liberal education. Curriculum decisions become purely political: departments simply demand "their share of the core," or curriculum committees restructure the core purely on the basis of comparison with other "attractive" schools, or students pressure for fashionable courses which seem "relevant."

In a day when many schools are losing their philosophical moorings, it would be a move in the direction of greatness for mainline liberal arts colleges in America and equivalents elsewhere to retain theirs. They should retain them not nominally, but with a conscientious search for philosophical identity. Lately, there is a noticeable swing of interest back to liberal education and the humanities, partly as preparation for coping with an ever-changing job market and partly as preparation for a fuller human life.[4] In fact, if current trends continue, the strong liberal arts institutions, often stereotyped as conservative, will end up being the true pioneers.

Since a single curriculum format cannot be unilaterally prescribed, each institution will have to work out exactly what courses it understands to be most faithful to the great heritage of liberal education and the humanities. However, a college need not strive for a core curriculum which is overly general, but only one general to the extent that it adequately acquaints students with the great ideas and lasting values of humankind as well as transmits the essential skills of continued learning. This is the way to construct a liberal education which is general in the sense of ranging over a number of subjects, but is quite specialized in the sense of focusing on the major themes and discoveries of civilization. In the long run, such an approach to liberal education will far surpass other approaches.

The Integration of Faith and Learning
The tradition of liberal education, with roots in both Hellenistic and Judeo-Christian thought, claims not only that there is a real and good world, but that knowledge about it is a consistent and unified whole. Liberal education, then, seeks to display the relationships between truths in the various fields of knowledge.

Explicitly Christian liberal education claims not just that the various areas of knowledge are integrated in its program, but that all areas of knowledge are somehow integrated with the Christian faith. Various types of Christian schools claim this kind of integration, but the categories in which it is currently discussed come largely from the literature on Christian higher education.

Christian theism holds that God created many kinds of reality about which there are whole domains of truth. The eternal God knows all of these truths; but it is our task to discover some of them in temporal life. A theistic position on the integration of knowledge can be explained in the following way. First, areas of knowledge are integrated with one another in that they all make best sense when they are firmly planted on the assumptions that reality is orderly, rational and moral. Second, domains of knowledge are integrated when each one, in its own distinct way, sheds light on the nature of the world and the human quest. And, third, knowledge is integrated when it is seen that what happens in one sphere of human endeavor has an impact on other spheres, that the human endeavor is not fragmented.

The integration of faith and knowledge can be defined as follows. First, faith is integrated with knowledge when it can be shown that the metaphysical, epistemological and axiological assumptions which make best sense of established knowledge are inherent in the Christian world view. Second, faith is integrated with knowledge when it is seen that the conclusions and insights of the various branches of inquiry are God's provision for our learning more about him and his world. Third, the appropriate integration occurs when the values and convictions of the Christian life are used to evaluate certain aspects of human knowledge. Fourth, faith and knowledge are integrated when our best information and insights are employed to help refine our understanding of Christianity. Fifth, faith is integrated with knowledge when learning is sought as something which can be used in

God's service. Arthur Holmes further elaborates on the concept of integration of faith and learning, stating that the motivation for study and learning can be distinctively Christian and that the context or community within which learning takes place can be founded on Christian principles.[5]

In all of the talk about integration, we must be careful to protect the integrity of each area of knowledge when it is supposedly being related to others. The desire to integrate all domains of knowledge has led some institutions to introduce a spate of "interdisciplinary courses" or "integrative studies." Typically introduced into the core curriculum in the name of liberal learning, such courses have tended to replace more solid and rigorous courses in separate, essential disciplines. Beginning students are required to learn very little about given fields of knowledge before they are asked to think about integrating them. Too often the result has been a superficial attempt at integration which deceives the students into thinking that they understand the subject better than they really do. As one critic put it, such courses usually degenerate into "sharing among the mutually uninformed." Robert Paul Wolff asserts that the lesson to be gained from the brief history of these courses is that integration is not a starting point but an achievement. It is only after students learn something well, some discipline or methodology, that they can sensitively and intelligently relate it to other branches of knowledge.[6]

Some educational thinkers propose, therefore, that we should not thrust relatively inexperienced college students into high-sounding integrative courses, but rather should attempt to get them to integrate their learning later in their college career.[7] Integrative efforts will be more effective after students have studied some of the solid disciplines of liberal learning, developed the appropriate skills of thinking and learning, explored the available life options, sampled various fields through elective courses (or course options), and formulated some intelligent opinions. In other words, the later years of college would be ideal for attempts at integration. These attempts could include seminars on topics and problems, interdisciplinary studies and so forth. In any event, the integrity of the disciplines involved must be respected, and no cheap and easy patterns of integration should be allowed.

A parallel concern can be raised about preserving the integrity of both the Christian faith and the knowledge with which it is integrated. E. Harris Harbison raises the issue in the form of a dual question: "Can a liberal education be a Christian education—and (vice versa) can a Christian education be a liberal education?"[8] Liberal education is founded upon the openness to truth and rational persuasion. The Christian faith involves a commitment to a certain set of beliefs and way of life. It might appear, therefore, that a liberal education is straitjacketed by the Christian world view and that unswerving commitment to Christianity is jeopardized by a liberal education which is always open to new truth.

Not all liberal education can be Christian. As long as a liberal education is simply conceived of as a broad one in which a variety of viewpoints are equally valid, then commitment to the definitive character of Christianity is impossible. As long as an education's only creed is a vague humanism and its main goal is to navigate effectively in society, then the Christian view will not completely illuminate its course of studies. Hence, this model of liberal education, which is essentially the rhetorical one discussed earlier, cannot enter into a fruitful relationship with the Christian faith.

However, the dialectical model of liberal education promises hope. The dialectical approach assumes that truth is available, that persons have dignity and that moral duty provides practical guidance—all affirmations of Christian theism. In a manner of speaking, liberal education—which ponders the significance of the human enterprise and explores the wonders of nature—is learning in search of a world view. It is indeed the Christian world view, which holds that there is a personal and moral deity whose creation education studies, that ultimately puts everything in perspective. Apart from the Christian faith, liberal education can only sense and long for this superior meaning. Ironically, liberal education, with its ideal of complete understanding, may forever fall short of its own goal unless enlightened by Christianity.

In order to be Christian, an educational institution need not curtail the presentation of diverse points of view, prohibit the debate of controversial topics, or restrict the direction of conscientious scholarship. Actually, a Christian institution of higher learning should be the most aggressive of all institutions in seeking open encounter with opposing views, stimulating creativity and searching for understanding. Where better to expose error than in a climate devoted to truth? Where better to evoke creative activity than in a place which appreciates the source of all creation? And where better to seek a wider understanding of the Christian faith than in a setting which seeks wisdom from all areas of life and thought? Education conducted in this manner can be thoroughly Christian without losing its integrity. Indeed, a version of the Christian faith which is neither dogmatic nor paranoid and which has a proper theory of Christian liberty can be both the ground and the fulfillment of liberal learning.

Not all Christian education can be properly liberal or liberating. We should be suspicious of institutions which promise a specifically Christian curriculum, or offer courses in "Christian sociology" or "Christian biology," or even promise to give the Christian view of every subject and issue. Such programs tend to be instruction-in-the-faith, aimed primarily at perpetuating the beliefs of a particular sect, and compromise the intellectual dignity of various fields in the name of religious insight. In both subtle and overt ways, such programs drive in, but do not draw out; they demand conformity, but do not invite free response;

they transmit information, but do not cultivate critical thinking. In short, there is instruction, but not education—and certainly not *liberal education* in any broad sense of the term.

One key to a Christian education which is truly *liberal*, or *liberating*, is humility. The acquisition of knowledge in all fields is an ongoing process in which final answers are not always available. Therefore, we must avoid the presumption that the Christian revelation somehow provides more ready answers than it does. Another key is fidelity to the research and methods of given fields of knowledge as God's provisions for our continued learning. Commitment to this kind of intellectual integrity is an outgrowth of Christian piety, not subversive to it. Such an approach to Christian education rests on the conviction that genuine knowledge, honestly gained through discipline and hard work, will shed light on religious faith and even correct misunderstandings of it. This is the sense in which a Christian education can be a liberal one.

Education in Morals and Values

As John Childs has stated, "Deliberate education is never morally neutral. A definite expression of preference for certain human ends, or values, is inherent in all efforts to guide the experience of the young."[9] In fact, the very existence of formal schooling reflects the conviction that parents and society must rear their young in appropriate ways, transmitting important information to them and encouraging certain patterns of behavior in them. It is inevitable, therefore, that the specific moral preferences of a school permeate its activities: the subjects chosen for study, the way they are taught, the playground rules and countless teacher-pupil transactions. The subject of education in morals and values becomes complicated in a secular and pluralistic society because of competing preferences. This line of discussion will be explored in the next chapter.

There are two extreme views of the relation of morality and

education. The first position, that education should be value neutral, has validity only in certain contexts. Many who hold this notion rightly guard against indoctrination and champion the right of students to make free choices. But some embrace the fallacious dualism between fact as objective truth and value as subjective preference, or at least the dichotomy that fact can be taught and character can in no way be taught. The second position identifies knowledge and virtue. Those who hold this position believe that theoretical knowledge translates into practical action, such that knowing the right is a sufficient condition for doing the right. While this classical position is too strong (ignoring such factors as knowledgeable and willful wrongdoing), it does recognize that there is much that education can do to foster moral life.

Between the two extremes described above, there is a moderate position which holds that education can influence moral development in at least two important ways. First, education can have a direct influence on moral growth by helping to shape the will, inculcating proper habits and dispositions. Second, education can have an indirect influence on the moral life of students by enlightening the mind, establishing the conviction that certain principles are approvable and certain kinds of actions right. Even on this middle view, there is the matter of specifying exactly what constitutes the moral life and determining what procedures are appropriate for developing it in students.

A full-blown Christian theism cites the Scriptures of both the Old and New Testaments as well as the moral experience of humankind as being major sources of moral ideals. According to Christian theism, the morally mature person has been liberated from the egocentrism of childhood and endeavors to live a life of love and respect for God, other persons and nature. As Aristotle observed, the mature and rational moral life must be entered through the avenue of habit and tradition. Young children are not fully capable of rational persuasion in the realm of morality and must gradually be brought to moral maturity through methods appropriate to their level of understanding.

A sophisticated Christian theism will extract advice from the best research into our natural moral nature. The current literature on the concept of moral development offers a number of theories. There are maturational theories (of Carl Rogers, Raths and Simon) which stress self-expression, and socialization theories (of Emile Durkheim and B. F. Skinner) which recommend conditioning the child to his or her social role. And there are cognitive-stage theories (of Jean Piaget and Lawrence Kohlberg) which emphasize the increasingly sophisticated patterns of moral reasoning through which a child advances, and thus probably qualify as a species of maturational theory.

The work of Piaget and Kohlberg has been used as a basis of the popular values-clarification movement. This approach attempts to get the student to become more aware of his or her own value-commitments. The typical procedure for accomplishing this is the presentation of a moral dilemma which students must contemplate and resolve. The pattern of reasoning which students use in this process will be characteristic of their stage of moral development: pre-conventional, conventional or post-conventional. Through the use of increasingly complicated problems, the teacher tries to stimulate students to progress to higher levels of moral reasoning.[10]

While there are some benefits in this particular approach to moral education, it suffers from a number of liabilities. Values-clarification strategy, along with most other contemporary moral-development strategies, fails to recognize any objective standard of moral responsibility. They all elevate either the individual or society to the status of supreme arbiter of values. Moreover, current theories fall remarkably short on the matter of teaching responsible action, since they fixate on cognitive and developmental factors.

A refreshing alternative in the field of moral education has been offered by Nicholas Wolterstorff, who addresses the question of how we can get children to internalize correct moral standards and act on them.[11] Calling his position a "responsibility theory," Wolterstorff judiciously navigates through the contemporary research and concludes that the best way to develop moral agents is to employ intelligent forms of discipline and modeling combined with explanations and reasons for why certain actions are right or wrong.

One important theme throughout Wolterstorff's study is that moral learning occurs in both cognitive and behavioral domains. Preferred methods try not simply to get the learner to reason with moral categories and principles, but also to act in accord with the beliefs he or she holds. Conversely, the learner's behavior must not simply be in conformity with accepted standards, but must be motivated by his or her own inward endorsement of those standards. Hence, it is paramount that discipline be administered with fairness and love, that reasons be given for it, that models earn the respect of the children and enunciate the moral principles on which they act, and that there be ample practice in reasoning from general moral principles to specific applications. Even the appearance of legalism and authoritarianism must be carefully avoided.

In light of the foregoing account, the question of whether moral education should be a separate subject or a dimension of all subjects is not extremely difficult. To be a place of real moral learning, the school, at a minimum, must be a moral community. This means that morality is encouraged in extracurricular activities and that moral issues are given serious consideration whenever they arise in any class. Although there may be helpful classes for certain kinds of moral education, nothing can substitute for a whole environment which is permeated by opportunities for moral learning. Excessive moralizing, however, should never be confused with moral education, as it shows disrespect for the learner's ability to understand reasonable and sensitive presentations of moral matters.

Obviously, the methods of teaching morally responsible action must be adapted to the learner's stage of mental and emotional development. For example, in the elementary grades, a structured environment and an overt system of rewards and punishments is appropriate. By contrast, use of extrinsic inducements becomes questionable at the college level, since they are associated with a lower stage of moral development than that desired of young adults. Moral education at this stage will have to make the most of its appeal to the reasonableness and worthwhileness of morality. At all levels, it is important that there be a learning environment in which mutual respect and support is present. Only within such a framework can there be optimum moral growth, for it makes possible increased apprehension of moral principles, encourages acting on those principles and even allows room for some moral mistakes along the way.

The ultimate goal of moral education is, of course, moral maturity, which is usually characterized in terms of the student's acquiring certain virtues corresponding to moral principles and being disposed to act morally on the basis of proper motives. An adequate Christian view recognizes another element of moral maturity: the student's being able to discuss and question the values which he or she has been taught. Naturally, the complete ability to do this is not present in younger children, but should be allowed to develop and not be stifled. This is essentially what Kant meant when he discussed the *autonomous* stage of moral living—not that the ego is the sole source of moral knowledge, but that one must appropriate what is moral for oneself, lucidly and rationally.

The rational stage of moral living involves agents' being able to ponder the credentials of the moral principles they have been taught, see the interrelationships and even rank them. It involves their being able to sort out the transcendent and lasting meaning of moral principles from their different concrete expressions in the lives of people and cultures. Although this ability to evaluate moral rules sometimes surfaces in simple questions of children, at the high-school and college levels the process of independent, rational thought generally becomes intense. It is paramount that the environment of moral learning not discourage or divert this activity in young adults.

Drawing a parallel to Michael Oakeshott's distinction between the "literature" and the "language" of a discipline, R. S. Peters says that moral education must first acquaint children with the forms of behavior, precepts, and principles of morality and then help them to become ever more skillful in their application and evaluation.[12] Just as students of geography must early learn the locations of the seas and continents, and mountains and plains before the concepts of space, time and distance can be grasped, young students of morality, so to speak, must first learn to go through the motions of ethical living before they can internalize its most cherished values.

The process of moral education is that of trying to help the "outsider" become an "insider." Aristotle masterfully explained it this way:

> But the virtues we get by first exercising them, as also happens in the case of the arts as well. For the things we have to learn before we can do them, we learn by doing them, for example, men become builders by building and lyre players by playing the lyre; so do we become just by doing just acts, temperate by doing temperate acts, brave by doing brave acts. . . . It makes no small difference, then, whether we form habits of one kind or another from our very youth; it makes a great difference or rather all the difference.[13]

So the door of the nursery is the gateway to moral education, and the school is the courtyard. The notion that one must first become a morally good person in order to perform morally good actions does not take into account this fact about our creaturehood. An adequate theory of moral education is much more sensitive to the interplay between being and doing.

Pedagogy and the Educational Enterprise

Although learning can and does take place outside of school and without the aid of a teacher, the role of the teacher is critical in the enterprise of formal education. Whether teachers function in a secular or religious setting, Christian theism has much to say about the aims and methods of their vocation. Discussing the nature of teaching, Philip Phenix asserts,

> Teaching is an act of creation and thus falls within that aspect of religion concerned with beginnings. The teacher participates in a making of persons. . . . It is a sacred responsibility to have a hand in fashioning human personalities, the highest of all the orders of created beings. Linked with creation is also destiny, for upon the manner of the teacher's creating depends the future of mankind.[14]

Certainly teaching is an art and the teacher is something of an artist. But teaching does not resemble arts such as painting or sculpture. And if teachers are artists then they do not resemble painters or sculptors who impose a preconceived form on a passive medium, be it color or clay. The art of teaching must rather be compared to the art of medicine. The teacher works with the inner principles of human nature in somewhat the same way as the physician works with the physical principles of health. Just as the physician attempts to get the body to the point where it can heal itself, the teacher must help bring students to the point at which they can learn on their own.

Jacques Maritain refers to the teacher as a "ministerial agent" in the educational process.[15] This terminology is rich with nuance for a Christian view of pedagogy. Teachers do not so much impart something of their own creation, but try to draw out the natural abilities of the learner. They are like mediators of something which is higher than themselves, helping others acquire not only the facts and skills, but also the dispositions and qualities suitable for rational beings in the image of God.

In a Christian view, then, the aims of teaching are based on the nature of reality, particularly the special reality which humanity is. The task of the teacher is conditioned by the right of students to develop their God-given capabilities. The goals of socialization for instrumentalism, autonomous choice for existentialism, order for naturalism and mental alertness for idealism—none of these quite expresses the aim of education as Christian theism envisions it. These other goals are included in but subordinate to the larger goal of human liberation in the image of God for which the teacher must strive.

It is not enough to point out incorrect opinions and claims. To liberate students from error and falsehood we must also help them to identify the underlying dispositions which create and nourish such opinions. Egocentrism, prejudice and sloth merely begin the list of traits which never give truth a fair chance. Of course, liberation *from* error and falsehood must be linked with liberation *to* truth. But teachers cannot be content to have students dutifully memorize a list of important truths any more than they can rest when the students can recite a list of falsehoods to be avoided. Teachers must strive to cultivate in pupils those traits and dispositions which are accommodating to truth. This means that in addition to the love of truth and the fundamental honesty which accompanies it, teachers must stimulate tendencies toward logical thinking, conscientiousness and tolerance, as well as implanting and nourishing a mentality which is supportive of the life of the mind.

All of this has very clear spiritual significance. The biblical tradition teaches that we worship and serve God not simply from the depths of our spirits, but with our bodies and minds as well. Therefore, the teacher, the one who prepares the mind, is in a strategic position to influence the spiritual life of the learner. The priority which Judaism has placed on being wise and imparting wisdom is an outgrowth of this basic principle. Although

many commentaries claim that three Old Testament offices an-
ticipate something of the status of Jesus—prophet, priest and
king—it can be easily argued that there are in fact four. The
office of *wise man* was venerated in Jewish tradition. Of the four
offices, three were consummated and terminated in Jesus Christ,
whereas he still allowed himself to be called "teacher," or rabbi.[16]

To spiritualize the mission of teaching is not to exaggerate its
importance. Teaching deals with the very core of one's being, the
mind and its thoughts and aspirations. Insofar as the many duties of teaching point the mind toward truth, wholeness and
excellence, teaching is indeed a type of ministry or sacred office,
and learning is a kind of worship. What Philip Phenix calls
"explicit worship" involves the visible use of the symbols and the
overt participation in the acts familiar to a religious community.
Seldom does teaching include leading students or anyone else in
explicit worship. However, in the classroom and other pedagogical situations, the teacher as ministerial agent has the function
of leading others in "implicit worship," according to Phenix.
The teacher is to lead students into study as a reflection of their
ultimate concern and religious devotion. Without the appearance of any of the customary religious forms, the teacher has the
opportunity to place students in a position in which their intellects are illumined, their wills energized for good, and their
spirits suffused with new life. In these moments of true inspiration, worship occurs: "Such worship need not wait for special
times and places, knows no difference of public or private school
nor law of separation, requires no approved formulae, and re-
spects no subject matter divisions."[17]

The methods of teaching, argues B. P. Komisar, include "sun-
dry doings, showings, and sayings."[18] In fact, the list of intellectual acts involved in teaching is quite long: telling, drilling, explaining, demonstrating, describing, narrating, announcing,
reporting and so forth. Obviously what makes any of these intellectual acts *teaching* is not mere showing-and-telling. Some-

thing more makes showing-and-telling to be teaching. The question of how a host of intellectual acts become acts of teaching is explored in recent philosophical literature. The literature discusses the special "causal efficacy" which teaching might be said to have, the intentionality of teaching, the desired uptake on the part of the learner and so forth.[19] Although no final definition of the teaching concept has yet been formulated, anyone interested in pedagogy must seriously ponder its nature.

In a day when teaching machines and self-paced instruction manuals promise "faster, more efficient" learning, we must be particularly alert not to forfeit a high conception of teaching. There may well be certain types of factual materials or performance skills which students can learn through rather impersonal means. Each school and each educator will have to evaluate the extent to which these methods are appropriate. However, the personal dimension of teaching, which comes through ever so many particular pedagogical transactions, is perhaps the fundamental quality which we must refuse to relinquish. The model of persons interacting with developing persons is indispensable to a complete concept of pedagogy.

Students need not simply learn facts and skills; they also need to witness well-integrated personalities using such facts and skills. Moreover, students need to observe whole persons who are able to employ their education to deal with the realities of life. The words of Abraham Joshua Heschel are appropriate: "What we need more than anything else is not textbooks but text-people. It is the personality of the teacher which is the text that the pupils read, the text they will never forget."[20]

6

Issues in
Educational
Practice

Our philosophy of life not only shapes educational theory, but provides guidance for educational practice. Thus the most abstract and general commitments influence concrete educational decisions. Although it is seldom possible to deduce particular policies and practices from a set of philosophical assumptions alone, we can put our assumptions together with factual information as a basis for thinking about the issues.

Like any other comprehensive philosophy, a sound Christian view provides a framework for interpreting numerous practical matters. However, there is no monolithic set of conclusions which Christians must draw. There is room for healthy diversity among those holding the same basic beliefs. In the present chapter, the emerging Christian orientation toward education is applied to the issues of liberal education and vocational training, public and private education, academic rights and freedoms, and teaching and indoctrination. A brief discussion of such subjects should be just the beginning of further exploration of these and other practical issues and options.

Liberal Education and Vocational Training

The philosophy of Christian theism endorses both the intrinsic value and the utility value of knowledge. On the one hand, knowledge is important because it helps us understand and develop our God-given humanity. On the other hand, knowledge is useful: it can help us get along in God's creation. A complete Christian view of education encompasses both aspects of knowledge. These two orientations toward knowledge have come to be embodied in two different educational formats: liberal education and practical (or career) training. A continual controversy rages as to whether these two models of education should be kept separate or whether they can be meaningfully related in a coherent system of schooling.

The problem with practical or vocational training, considered entirely on its own terms, lies in the type of person it tends to produce, the type of mentality and orientation toward life which it can foster. Career training suits a person for satisfactory functioning in the job market. While recognizing the legitimacy of work and productivity in society, a Christian perspective indicates that life is more than employment, and people are more than the job they can do.[1] A purely vocational approach does little toward enlightening the student to the enduring issues and great ideas of human civilization. It offers virtually nothing to awaken the student to his or her own unique potentialities as a human being. Furthermore, it is not essentially aimed at stirring a consciousness of social duty and religious service.

Jacques Maritain calls purely vocational training a "servile education" and contrasts it with a "liberal education."[2] The Latin term for liberal is *libere*, which means "to free." Historically this meaning applied to the free men of state who were capable of self-governance. A liberal education liberates, then, by freeing the mind from ignorance and prejudice, and strengthening it to think and judge. Although in our day there is no longer legalized slavery, the danger of another kind of slavery still exists—slavery to self-interest, impulse and emotion. There is nothing inherent in a vocational or technical education which counteracts the kind of mental slavery that threatens a society increasingly interested in comfort, pleasure and acquisition.

Without denigrating the need for gainful employment or the need to receive training for it, the tradition of liberal education has always attempted to enable students to become leaders. It has not been interested simply in training the functionaries of society. Since it is imperative that the modern world be permeated by Christians who can think, who are sensitive to the enduring questions of life, who can formulate plans and instill vision, and who can intelligently persuade others of the adequacy of Christ for the human condition, liberal education—the humanities and the sciences—must be taken seriously. Liberal education is intimately concerned with the same issues that Christianity addresses: the meaning of life, the nature of values, the shape of human history and the contours of the world order.

Liberal education does not apply only to the college level. Adler and others have correctly pointed out that the concept of liberal education is appropriate for all levels of schooling and for all ages.[3] He decries the "abominable discrimination" which lies at the heart of our system of public or state education, saying that it offers two divergent tracks to growing students, the vocational and the liberal, the technical and the humanities. Students, particularly at the high-school stage, are slotted along these tracks, often by formal evaluation and teacher encouragement, sometimes by their own choosing. Adler's proposal for a liberal education for all public or state school students, penned on behalf of the Paideia Group, boldly recommends teaching all children the indispensable skills of learning and exposing them to those concepts and experiences which can awaken their full humanity. Although some children will be able to handle more liberal learning than others, the Paideia Group still advocates providing quality liberal education to all.

Since the process of self-definition is especially acute during the years of late adolescence and young adulthood, the consideration of liberal learning during these stages is very significant. Whether students attend a state university or a private college, they should seek a dimension of liberal learning in their formal education. Although there are a number of large universities in which a liberal education is officially offered, most have drifted away from any potent liberal arts program. This places a heavier burden on the student to select courses and read books which provide elements of liberal learning.

Public and Private Education
The respective roles of the public and private sectors in education have long been debated. Historically, this issue closely parallels the question of state and church involvement in education. Although some issues regarding private involvement are not related to religion, the following treatment will focus largely on the church and state controversy as it exists in the United States. But the principles involved certainly have wider application.

One starting point for Christian thinking on this issue is the nature of children as God's creatures, with the right of fulfilling their capacities to think freely and act responsibly. Education, of course, is a vehicle through which these capacities can be developed. Based on this unique nature, then, children have a right to be properly educated. While education takes place in many areas of life, formal schooling provides an important source of education.

The rub comes with the question of who may, or should, provide formal schooling for our youth. Superseding bygone ages when only an elite could attend school, the American experiment in democracy has entrenched the conviction that the state has the right, even the duty, to support all levels of education.[4] A similar view is found in Britain and in most Western democracies. It is not simply for mental, moral and spiritual growth that the school needs to exist, but also for the overall good of civil society. If democracy is going to work, then there must be adequate preparation for citizenship. Since Christian theism endorses the principles of justice and liberty which undergird constitutional democracy, it supports the right of government to educate its citizens.

Controversy arises when the role of government is improperly interpreted. For example, compulsory school attendance laws are justifiable, but it is not fair for a government to require that all children attend public or state schools. When the Oregon legislature passed a law in 1922 requiring every child between the ages of eight and eighteen to attend public school, this issue became acute. In 1925, the United States Supreme Court struck down the Oregon law as unconstitutional. The court decision recognized the right of parochial and other private schools to exist alongside public or state schools. Of course the state reserves the right to inspect all schools according to its educational standards. A similar right exists, for example, in Holland, where there is a strong emphasis on nonstate schooling.

A long string of decisions regarding public and private involvement in the schooling of our youth has followed this early Supreme Court decision (regarding released time for religious instruction, school prayer and Bible reading, and so on). Many of these decisions relate to the constitutional doctrine of separation of church and state. Since the public role in education has grown from local or community control to state supervision and even federal involvement, the issues have become increasingly complicated.

Additional complications are due to the diversity of modern American and Western European life—in moral, religious and other areas. Whereas the political consensus about the need for public or state education once coincided with a significant religious consensus among the populace, now pluralism generates new and conflicting pressures on education. Thinking Christians must find meaningful ways of understanding our current situation and living in a society in which homogeneity of belief and lifestyle will probably never again exist.

Without denigrating America's rich spiritual and moral legacy from the Judeo-Christian heritage, contemporary American Christians need to reconsider the relation of church and state. Secular dogmatists, at one extreme, insist that the government heavily regulate and tax churches and other private educational organizations, with the ultimate result of eroding their freedom and independence. Religious zealots, at the other extreme, demand that public forms of education recognize that America is traditionally a "Christian nation" and teach in accord with that tradition, with the eventual result of imposing this view on those who do not hold to Christian belief. Milder parallels to this latter view exist also in Great Britain among some Conservatives.

Neither of these extreme positions is reasonable, and neither is faithful to the original meaning of the First Amendment to the Constitution of the United States: "Congress shall make no law respecting an establishment of religion, or prohibiting the free exercise thereof." The ultrasecularist, in effect, wants to give the state the power to kill religion. The religious crusader, in effect, desires that the state have the power to advance religion. But the classical doctrine of separation denies that the state should have the power either to inhibit or to promote religion.[5]

The constitutional doctrine reflects the wisdom that government and church can function best without excessive entanglement with one another. It also protects the free exercise of religion to the extent that it does not infringe on the liberties of others. Naturally, Christians will not want the state to monitor their faith. It is more likely that they will err, perhaps unconsciously, in wanting government to show favoritism.

Although governmental favor may initially seem desirable, it presents a number of hidden dangers. For one thing, the official recognition of a religion by a public organization or agency tends to become purely perfunctory and rote. Psychological research shows that nominal agreement with a religious position, whether indicated by the meaningless recitation of prayers or other routine exercises, tends to damage real religious growth. Hence believers ought to covet for themselves and their particular church the exclusive religious instruction and nurture of their children and be wary about the public endorsement of any particular religion. For another thing, once the precedent is set, govenmental favoritism of one religious faith can eventually change to governmental favoritism of another faith. Hence, it is wise to promote the establishment of a neutral state which accepts the clash of views on religion, ethics and a host of other matters. In *The Idea of a Secular Society and Its Significance for Christians,* D. L. Munby explores alternative models for the state and society. He concludes that a neutral state and society conform more closely to a Christian view of human life than any other pattern.[6] God-given humanity includes the right to judge what is true and good. Because of our finitude and fallibility in areas legitimately left to reason, conscience and taste, the principle of not imposing the preference of some on others is valid. Besides, truth itself may be more fairly treated when a variety of opinions is allowed to flourish. If reasons for a belief are correct, let them stand in the midst of dynamic interchange with competing beliefs.[7]

From the point of view of Christian theism, then, a good case can be made for establishing public or state schools and protecting private and religious schools. Decisions about whether to attend or to send one's children to attend a public or private school must be made on an individual basis.[8] In some cases, the choice may be for the public or state educational system. This selection can be influenced by financial ability. It can also be affected by how important it seems for the child to rub shoulders with the common lot of humanity and find out how to manage in a pluralistic setting. In other cases, the choice may be for a private school setting. This decision might be influenced by how needful it is for the student to be in a protected or "pure" environment from a religious point of view or to avoid decidedly antireligious teachings in a public or state school. And it can be based on the conviction that communication of Christian truths should be done within a total educational context which only a private institution can provide.

Certainly both parents and the church should communicate a Christian view of learning to children, whether the children attend public or private educational institutions. In working through all of these sorts of issues, it is important to remember the broad view of God, humanity and the world which Christianity projects and the principles of justice and fairness, for both oneself and others, which it implies.

Academic Rights and Freedoms

The educational enterprise rests on certain concepts of the rights and duties of the members of the academic community, whether at the elementary or university level. An examination of the concepts related to academic freedom and responsibility provides a deeper understanding of the educational quest and reveals that Christian theism offers a solid basis for its integrity.

Although many American educational experts say that the doctrine of academic freedom is simply derived from the Bill of Rights, it is far more than this. Of course teachers in a school or college are protected by the same constitutional guarantees of freedom of thought and speech that protect every American citizen. However, the doctrine of academic freedom implies that an institution of learning be endowed with certain rights which do not belong, for example, in a business enterprise or government bureau. Perhaps this fundamental doctrine had its origin in Socrates' eloquent defense of himself against the charge of corrupting the youth of Athens. In any case, it has had a continuous history from the beginning of universities in the twelfth century up to the present.[9]

The premise of such thinking is the preciousness of the search after truth. There should be not only appropriate honor for the scholars who commit themselves to this search and for the teachers who lead others in it, but also a system of protections for their activity. In both medieval and modern times, tenure has been affirmed, not to promote job security among one class of professionals, but to protect the nature of the academic enterprise.[10] Since the search after truth can be damaged by those wielding political power, the positions of proven scholars and teachers who hold unpopular views may be threatened by administrators and pressure groups.[11] Academic freedom is not meant to prevent the removal of a tenured teacher when there is flagrant debasing of the academic mission through either incompetence or immorality.

The concept of academic freedom involves the traditional "mystique" of freedom and honor.[12] It essentially entails the teacher's freedom to study and do research, and to speak and write about the results of that study and research. The idea applies in much the same way, although with some qualification, to students. The learned scholar has the full academic authority and rights which pertain to the possession of expertise; the rawest student merely has the right of exploration. In both cases, but at different levels, academic freedom may be defined as the freedom to think for oneself, to consider ideas, to make errors and correct them, to communicate the results of one's study, and to disagree with others on reasonable grounds. Despite the fact that Christian theism affirms the dignity of all people and of all legitimate work, it assigns knowledge and wisdom an extremely high status and cherishes the role of those who seek it.

The rights of the teacher or scholar are necessarily correlated with those of the student or learner. The academic freedom of teachers or professors or lecturers is not the privilege of espousing just any opinion they please, or of teaching views outside their spheres of competence. Where there is the prior commitment to truth, there is a responsibility placed on educators to try to determine truth in their fields and to communicate it fairly to students. The commitment to truth also supports the students' equally important right not to be indoctrinated, misled or incompetently taught. None of this precludes diversity of judgment about facts and values; it simply upholds the dignity of the mind in the search after truth.

Historically the principle of academic freedom has been threatened by those who pressure for restrictive legalism and those who crusade for unbridled license. The former group includes many people who do not understand the nature of an academic community: citizen censorship committees which know little about reading, lay boards of trustees which panic when controversial subjects are discussed on campus, administrations which attempt to abolish tenure, and government agencies which discriminate against religious belief in the name of separation of church and state. All pose dangers to academic freedom. Such parties have often wanted to limit the liberty of thought and discussion in ways injurious to the educational enterprise.

Legitimate intellectual liberty has also been threatened by those with the opposite orientation that any opinion or action whatever should be protected under the canopy of academic freedom. Actions which are immoral, practices which are subversive, and positions which are incompetent have been erroneously brought under the canopy of academic freedom. This amounts to stretching the very precise concept of academic freedom to imply a *laissez faire* environment in which all views, and perhaps all actions, are viewed as having equal worth.

In order to find a balance between these two extremes, faculty and administration must work to build a structure of freedom for inquiry and expression—whether at a public or private, secular or religious school. Typically there will be a greater variety of opinion reflected among the staff and students of a public university. But their academic freedom must not be confused with the anarchy of opinion which frequently prevails.

Intellectual liberty is not automatically forfeited when an institution seeks to perpetuate its historic identity. After all, academic freedom promotes honesty and not total neutrality. The problem arises when an educational institution conceives too narrowly of what constitutes its identity or of what counts as student and faculty loyalty. When a school forgets that responsible persons can interpret or apply the same basic commitments somewhat differently, it mistakes sameness for safety. In the public arena, the *Scopes* v. *State* "monkey trial" is a prime example of mistaking a scientific opinion for theological heresy. Equally harmful mistakes have been made in private religious institutions where intelligent and dedicated lecturers and professors have been censured or dismissed for expressing views which do not echo narrow "party line" language.

Without a doubt, truth sometimes needs a helping hand.[13] But before a helping hand is given, all of an institution's constituents, both internal and external, must distinguish grievous abuse of academic liberty from desirable diversity of opinion. The principle of academic freedom demands that as much diversity be allowed as is consistent with the identity and aims of the institution, even one with a specific religious identity. In the course of things, it is wise to allow errors in belief and unpopular opinions to exist, because the evil of suppressing them is almost always greater than the evils they present. Building a rather monolithic climate of opinion and belief is not only stifling to the minds of those living within it, but also robs a tradition of positive input and constructive criticism.

A sound version of Christian theism endorses the lofty ideal of academic freedom. It affirms the dignity of the mind in the image of God and the reality of a knowable world. Recognizing our finiteness and fallibility, Christian theism denies that any person or organization can have inerrant knowledge or final truth and denounces any attempt to demand conformity of belief. Belief, intellectual assent, is like worship and faith; it cannot be coerced but must be freely given.[14] Christian theism concurs with the best traditional wisdom on the matter: there is simply no acceptable alternative to academic freedom.

Teaching and Indoctrination

It is fascinating to ponder the somewhat elusive differences between legitimate teaching and dangerous indoctrination. James McClellan offers four criteria for making the distinction: content, intent, method and control.[15] First, the content of teaching must primarily be the subject matter and judicious appraisals of it. When the content of instruction is drawn from doctrinal systems or ideologies which either have not been or cannot be proved through the methods of the field in question, or at least given reasonable argument, then there is risk of indoctrination. An ideology in the present sense rigidly asserts its beliefs and refuses to be self-critical. There is nothing necessarily dangerous, however, in drawing from a system of beliefs which welcomes open discussion and evaluation.

Second, the intent of teaching must be to discover and transmit truth in a way appropriate to the nature of the mind of the learner. When the intent of instruction, held at whatever degree of self-consciousness, is to get pupils to believe a certain claim, then that intent could shape every aspect of teacher-student interaction into a form of indoctrination. If the aim is continually to smooth over doubts and secure credence rather than to bring pupils to a point at which they can judge truth from error for themselves, then the academic enterprise has been compromised. Obviously a kind of open relativism, which is typically disinterested in what pupils believe, is not protection against indoctrination. The intent to get pupils to believe something may sometimes be appropriate. But the intent must be balanced by a number of other factors, including their need to develop the power of independent judgment.

Third, the method of instruction must be one which strengthens the powers of reason and discrimination. Whenever intrinsically good methods such as lecture or drill on predigested material are used consistently without being balanced by exercises in creative and independent thought, then indoctrination is possible. The techniques of contemporary religious cults (such as severing normal family and social bonds, repetitious chanting, obedience to a guru figure) are methods of indoctrination.

Fourth, the element of control is a little-researched factor in distinguishing genuine teaching from indoctrination. Teaching can lapse into indoctrination when, within the social system where it occurs, the instructor is presumed to have the power and the right to reward or punish students for their success or failure in accepting the beliefs that are being communicated, and perhaps for their behavior in general. Again, Christian educators and educational institutions should take stock of this fact. It is not necessarily the falsity of a belief but its manner of transmission that makes its propagation indoctrination.

If students have the right not to be indoctrinated, then teachers, administrators and parents have the duty to monitor the potential of indoctrination within the educational experience. As Lord Acton remarked, "at the root of all liberty is the liberty to learn." At the heart of the liberty of learning is the distinction between substantive beliefs and canons of thought by which to evaluate those beliefs.[16] Any opinion or view is subject to rational scrutiny; and no belief should be recommended or adopted without rational persuasion taking place in a way appropriate to the maturity of the learner. Teachers who respect this Socratic principle will not be indoctrinators. By the same token, students would show more respect for their own intellectual rights and greatly reduce the risk of being indoctrinated, if they would not treat knowledge as something that can be passively received, but pursue it as something to be earned by diligent effort.

7

Christianity and the Pursuit of Excellence

A Christian world view beckons us to the pursuit of excellence in all things. Our divinely created nature tends toward fulfillment and longs for a measure of perfection in earthly life. Our witness to the world is enhanced by the care we put into our activities. And, our general Christian calling is satisfied by giving our best efforts as service to God.

The quest for excellence in education is a natural outgrowth of such motivations. There are additional motivations for excellence in education, corresponding to the intrinsic and utility values of knowledge. First, Christians have the philosophical basis for the inherent worth of knowledge and personal improvement. Education deals with the matters of the human mind and spirit, and thus activates a part of our nature which is like God. Second, for Christians, education can greatly aid the communication of the faith. It offers an understanding of people past and present, insight into their deep concerns which Christianity addresses, and methodologies for advancing the gospel.

Although the concept of excellence has an impact on Christian thinking about education at a number of points, the following sections discuss two important ones: whether education is viewed as a product or a process determines *the kind of excellence* which can be achieved; and how the ultimate goal of education is conceived determines its *lasting contribution*.

Education as Product and Process

To think of education exclusively in terms of curriculum structure and course content is to treat knowledge as a product for consumption. Some types of educational programs tend to do just this (vocational and technical training, for example). However, when the mission of education is broadened to include human liberation and fulfillment, treating knowledge as a product is inadequate. A vital principle of liberal education is that knowledge has another side: an active, dynamic, processive side. The sheer attainment of truth, say, through rote memorization or the recitation of prepackaged answers, is not enough. To speak of the knowledge *process* is to emphasize the aggressive search after truth, the exploration of ideas and the refinement of mental skills. Learning, then, is not a matter of static achievement, but of dynamic activity.

Whether an institution is Christian or not, if it intends to provide a holistic and liberal education, it must be concerned not merely with the propagation of truth, but with the impact of the search for truth on the student's mind. It is of supreme importance not simply *that* truth is found, but *how* it is sought. Truth is properly sought through honest and critical thinking. Students can think carefully only when they are exposed to great ideas, taught to be thorough and accurate, and helped to make mature judgments.

The integrity of the intellectual process is so important that some thinkers speak of an ethical responsibility which attaches to it. They claim that no person has the right to believe just anything at all, but is entitled to hold a belief after careful examination of the evidence. To explain this ethical requirement, W. K. Clifford, a nineteenth-century philosopher, tells a story of a shipowner who ignored reports that his old and deteriorating vessel was unsound. He told himself that it was seaworthy because it was originally well built and had made so many previous journeys. He acquired the belief that the ship was sound and allowed it to carry many immigrant families on the transatlantic voyage. The ship "went down in mid-ocean and told no tales."[1]

Rhetorically, Clifford asks what we shall say of the shipowner. Clearly, we shall say that he is guilty of the death of those people. Granted, the shipowner "sincerely" believed in the soundness of the ship, or so we are told in the hypothetical story. However, he believed in a manner which violates the ethics of the intellectual life. He "had no right to believe on such evidence as was before him"; he had acquired his belief by stifling doubts and avoiding close scrutiny of the facts. Clifford correctly indicates that even if we alter the story a bit and suppose that the ship was not unsound after all, the shipowner is still as guilty as before. The question of right or wrong here does not pertain to the actual truth or falsity of the belief, but to the way it is attained and held. John Stuart Mill makes this same point in his classic essay *On Liberty*. Mill states that the truth may reside in the mind as a prejudice, a superstition, and that this is beneath the dignity of a rational being.[2]

Now it may be that Clifford's specific formulation of the ethics of belief, along with what constitutes acceptable evidence, is overly stringent. It relies on a naturalistic model of rationality and thus tends to be prejudiced against religious belief. It also favors those who have high intellectual acumen and thus tends to be elitist. Yet these are not grounds to dismiss the notion that we are responsible for the way we form beliefs.

The basic emphasis that we must be responsible in what we

believe is consistent with Christian theism and is especially relevant in the educational enterprise. Certainly we are not obliged
to allow anti-Christian assumptions to dictate the criteria for
responsible believing. And we should not construct a model of
rational belief which supports intellectual elitism, making proper belief forever unattainable by countless sincere Christians.
Thoughtful Christians need to work toward a conception of the
rational process which gives a place to the need for intellectual
responsibility in religious belief and still makes sense of the way
numerous intellectually unsophisticated people come to God. At
the very least, a proper conception will endorse the divinely
created need to see our beliefs as being true and reasonable, and
recognize that people are required to seek the understanding
proportionate to their mental abilities.

A helpful account of responsible belief is needed both to
answer critics and to tutor the faithful. Clifford and other critics
accuse religious believers of violating the ethics of belief. We
need to consider carefully what really constitutes legitimate
grounds for belief, particularly regarding the ultimate issues of
life. Clifford's empirical approach distorts any inquiry of this
type. Unfortunately, some believers give critics the occasion to
charge them with irresponsible believing. Some believers have
become credulous persons, defending themselves by saying that
their religious belief is a purely private matter without any rational or ethical constraints. It is no wonder that nonbelievers
sometimes characterize believers as believing on fancy, ignoring
doubts, and directing their minds toward the comfortable and
the familiar.

Christians cannot allow themselves to acquiesce in the comfortable and the familiar, and thereby embrace a kind of provinciality which detracts from a greater understanding of Christianity and the world at large. Educators and students must be
especially careful to maintain the intellectual integrity of the
Christian faith. Suppose, for instance, that a college student

learns of some new and different ideas, particularly threatening to religion; and let us suppose that the student experiences doubt about his or her own religious commitment. The problem cannot be completely resolved by trying to have more faith. Eventually, the student must be encouraged to deal with these doubts in an intellectual process. If the doubts were acquired by thinking, then they must ultimately be eliminated by *thinking*. No amount of spiritual devotion, firm resolve, or sheer will power can eliminate them. The student must come to see Christianity to be valid in way appropriate to his or her level of intellectual understanding. The process of intellectually analyzing aspects of faith, as well as aspects of life in general, is risky. But risk is necessary to a truly free and responsible search after truth.[3]

While Christianity mandates that we are "to bring all thoughts into the captivity of Christ" (2 Cor 10:5), the theme of intellectual ethics permits only proper methods for doing so. There are many improper ways of taking thoughts captive or inducing belief: peer pressure, propaganda, hypnosis and drug therapy barely begin the list of unacceptable ways. However, to inculcate belief by insisting that such and such is what evangelicalism holds, or that thus and so is a comforting doctrine, or that good Christians always affirm X, is equally unacceptable.

A children's story by Madeleine L'Engle provides a gripping illustration of this point. *A Wrinkle in Time* depicts the situation of several children who find a way of traveling through space and time.[4] They embark on a rescue mission for their father, a scientist, who has been taken captive on a distant planet by a cosmic evil force. The emissary of evil on that planet is called "the man with red eyes," and the children know that they must face him to free their father. When they arrive on the planet, they find that the people there are organized and useful, even though unspontaneous and unresponsive, because of the influence of the man with red eyes. When confronted, the man with red eyes demands that they surrender to his will, letting him bear the burden of thought and decision for them. He promises to make them just like "all of the happy, useful people" on the planet, if they will succumb to his hypnotic power.

The man with red eyes may be interpreted as a type of *false Christ*. He called for the children to make what Michael Cain would call "psychic surrender."[5] However, no one should believe something because doing so will make him happy, useful, spiritual or anything else—but only because he sees it as true. The *real Christ* does not offer an end to intellectual hard work; he calls us right back to it.

In C. S. Lewis's *The Screwtape Letters*, Screwtape advises his nephew Wormwood not to employ *argument* to try to lead his victim to hell:

> The trouble with argument is that it moves the whole struggle onto the Enemy's own ground [here "Enemy" refers to God]. He can argue too; whereas in really practical propaganda of the kind I am suggesting he has been shown for centuries to be greatly the inferior of Our Father Below. By the very act of arguing, you awaken the patient's reason; and once it is awake, who can foresee the result. Even if a particular train of thought can be twisted so as to end in our favor, you will find that you have been strengthening in your patient the fatal habit of attending to universal issues and withdrawing his attention from the stream of immediate sense experiences. Teach him to call it "real life" and don't let him ask what he means by "real."[6]

The rest of this horrifying letter needs to be read in context. The message, however, is abundantly clear: God is the Lord of truth and argument, the Master of giving reasons. Christians should not fear the intellectual process, since intellect is an ally of genuine faith, not a nemesis.

There is absolutely no inconsistency between Christian commitment and the process of seeking truth. In fact, Christian theism affirms that one draws life from the other, that they are inseparably bound together. Commitment to Christ gives us a focus for truth; and concern for truth keeps us from accepting false substitutes for Christ. In *The Drama of Atheist Humanism*, Henri de Lubac suggests that one major fallacy of the modern age is not simply that it has rejected Christ, but that it has abandoned Socrates.[7] Pointing to Socrates as the epitome of the love of truth, de Lubac says that, as regard for objective, rational truth declines, commitment to Christ is caricatured as purely emotional or subjective. De Lubac might also have warned us of moderns who equate truth with scientific and empirical facts and thus remain blind to the larger truths of life. In either case, the possibility of maintaining Christianity as a true religion is undermined. Until our age recovers a regard for higher level truth and the intellectual process for seeking it, calls to genuine religious commitment may fall on deaf ears.

Distinctively Christian education must therefore help restore the love of truth and the earnest search after it.[8] There cannot be the slightest hint of a dichotomy between the intellectual life properly understood and the life of faith. Indeed, because of devotion to Christ, we should not merely endeavor to know the truth in whatever area it may be found, but to love the truth and to inspire others to love it too. After all, people are impelled not so much by what they *know*, but by what they *love*. And to love the truth is to love something of Christ.

For a school to fulfill its purpose, it must extend the idea of the search after truth, the process of seeking knowledge, to all facets of the student's experience. The whole climate of learning, including the religious and social dimensions, should be shaped and informed by the overarching desire for truth. If there are religious activities, they should maintain the intellectual credibility appropriate to an institution that values God's gift of the mind. The social structure and discipline must avoid undue arbitrariness and restrictiveness in order to allow room for the free and maturing choices of young people. Indeed the total environment must impart a sense of self-worth and mutuality, cultivate an awareness of large ideas and principles, and avoid pettiness and provinciality. The ideal is not simply to integrate knowledge with knowledge and knowledge with faith, but all aspects of life into a unified whole. The process of learning in such an environment can be a profoundly life-changing experience.

Intellect in the Service of Christ

Harry Blamires states that the goal of distinctively Christian education is the formation of a "Christian mind."[9] In his exploration of the characteristics of the Christian mind—an intelligence which thinks in categories which are distinctively Christian—he correctly focuses not on the need to develop persons who can think *and* who are also Christian, but on the need for those who can *think Christianly*.[10]

However, Blamires's concept of the "Christian mind," along with its defining characteristics, can be ramified to include all of the elements of personhood which Christian education should enhance. Hence, the total aim of Christian education is the formation of a "Christian person." This way of looking at the goal shows that it is not purely intellectual traits which Christian education should foster, but those of character as well. It is not enough to think Christianly; we must also be disposed to *act* Christianly. Christian education must seek to instill a sense of moral duty and a disposition to act responsibly in the world.

For Christians, education cannot be simply a badge or credential; it is our reasonable service. We cannot rest in the ultimate truth of Christianity and avoid seeking finite truths about the world it seeks to penetrate. If our mission is, so to speak, to help Christ save the world, then we must take seriously the complexity of the task. Bringing Christian redemption to human existence involves more than direct evangelization; it includes the search for truth and goodness in every sphere of life.

This scenario may seem hopelessly visionary. While it is visionary, it is not hopeless. Every person and every community must have an ideal toward which to strive. We may not always live up to our ideals, but their presence is of supreme importance. There is no ideal more exhilarating or more worthwhile than that of education in the service of Christ. It deserves the best that is in us: stewardship of our talents, excellence in our performances, honesty and rigor in our thinking. We need the ideal; we need to reflect on what it means to love God with all of our minds. For in this there is great hope!

Notes

Chapter 1: What Is Philosophy of Education?

[1]Dionysius of Halicarnassus *Aristotle* xi.

[2]Abraham Lincoln, "To the people of Sangamon Co.," March 9, 1832.

[3]Charles Silberman, *Crisis in the Classroom: The Remaking of American Education* (New York: Vintage Books, 1970), p. 11.

[4]Lawrence Cremin, *The Genius of American Education* (New York: Vintage Books, 1965), p. 30.

[5]For a fuller discussion of issues in metaphysics, see William Hasker, *Metaphysics: Constructing a World View* (Downers Grove, Ill.: InterVarsity Press, 1983).

[6]For a fuller discussion of issues in epistemology, see David Wolfe, *Epistemology: The Justification of Belief* (Downers Grove, Ill.: InterVarsity Press, 1982).

[7]For a fuller discussion of issues in ethics, see Arthur Holmes, *Ethics: Approaching Moral Decisions* (Downers Grove, Ill.: InterVarsity Press, 1984).

[8]For a fuller discussion of constructing a world view, see Arthur Holmes, *Contours of a World View* (Grand Rapids, Mich.: Eerdmans, 1983).

[9]Robert Beck, ed., *Perspectives in Philosophy: A Book of Readings,* 3d ed. (New York: Holt, Rinehart and Winston, 1964), p. 3.

Chapter Two: Traditional Philosophies of Education

[1]For a fuller discussion of the extent to which educational conclusions are deducible from philosophical premises, see Harry S. Broudy, "How Philosophical Can Philosophy of Education Be?" *Journal of Philosophy* 52 (October

1955): 612-22; Hobart Burns, "The Logic of 'Educational Implications,' " *Educational Theory* 12 (January 1962): 53-63; Joe Burnett, "An Analysis of Some Philosophical and Theological Approaches to Formation of Education-al Policy and Practice," *Proceedings of the Seventeenth Annual Meeting of the Philosophy of Education Society* (1961). Also, Burnett, "Some Observations on the Logical Implications of Philosophical Theory for Educational Theory and Practice," *Proceedings of the Fourteenth Annual Meeting of the Philosophy of Education Society* (1958): 51-57.

[2]For a discussion of criteria for evaluating world views, see Hasker, *Metaphys-ics.*

[3]William E. Hocking, *Types of Philosophy,* 3d ed. (New York: Scribner's, 1959), p. 152.

[4]In keeping with our microcosmic/macrocosmic model, we note that Kant wrote of the "systematic union of different rational beings by means of com-mon laws." Immanuel Kant, *The Fundamental Principles of the Metaphysic of Ethics,* trans. Otto Manthey-Zorn (New York: Appleton-Century-Crofts, 1938), pp. 50-51.

[5]Immanuel Kant, *Critique of Judgment,* trans. J. Bernard (London: Macmillan, 1982), pp. 153, 189-91.

[6]Herman H. Horne, "An Idealistic Philosophy of Education," in *Philosophies of Education: National Society for the Study of Education, Forty-first Yearbook,* part 1 (Chicago: University of Chicago Press, 1942), pp. 156-57.

[7]See William Frankena, *Three Historical Philosophies of Education: Aristotle, Kant, Dewey* (Glenview, Ill.: Scott, Foresman, 1965), pp. 83-97.

[8]J. Donald Butler, *Idealism in Education* (New York: Harper and Row, 1966), pp. 91-92.

[9]G. E. Moore, "The Refutation of Idealism," *Philosophical Studies* (1922), re-printed in M. Weitz, ed., *Twentieth-Century Philosophy: The Analytic Tradition* (New York: Macmillan, 1966), pp. 15-36.

[10]Immanuel Kant, *Education,* trans. A. Churton (Ann Arbor: University of Michigan Press, 1960), p. 77.

[11]Immanuel Kant, *Religion within the Limits of Reason Alone,* trans. T. M. Greene and H. H. Hudson (New York: Harper and Row, 1964), p. 3.

[12]Ernest Nagel, "Naturalism Reconsidered," in Beck, *Perspectives,* p. 191.

[13]Ibid., p. 196.

[14]Ibid., pp. 192-93. Also see Ernest Nagel, "Philosophy of Science and Edu-cational Theory," in Joe Park, ed., *Selected Readings in the Philosophy of Edu-cation,* 4th ed., (New York: Macmillan, 1974), pp. 113-20; here Nagel shows how analytic philosophy of science clarifies how we can justify normative judgments and reason with them to the ends of education.

[15]*The Humanist* (San Francisco: American Humanist Association, July-August 1968), inside front cover.

[16]B. F. Skinner, *Science and Human Behavior* (New York: Macmillan, 1953). Also see Skinner, *The Technology of Teaching* (New York: Appleton-Century-Crofts, 1968). Skinner's large-scale philosophical views are expressed in *Beyond Freedom and Dignity* (New York: Knopf, 1971).

[17]Harry Broudy, *Building a Philosophy of Education* (Englewood Cliffs, N.J.: Prentice-Hall, 1954), p. 405.

[18]Karl Marx, *Capital*, vol. 1 (New York: Modern Library, n.d.), pp. 436-40.

[19]Karl Marx, *Communist Manifesto*, in K. Marx and F. Engels, *Selected Works*, 2 vols. (Moscow: Foreign Languages Publishing House, 1962), 1:33-69.

[20]C. S. Lewis, *Miracles* (New York: Macmillan, 1946), chap. 3.

[21]For a fuller discussion of this kind of problem, see Nicholas Wolterstorff, *Educating for Responsible Action* (Grand Rapids, Mich.: Eerdmans, 1980), especially chap. 5.

[22]For further reading, see David Ross, *Aristotle*, rev. ed. (London: University Paperbacks, 1964).

[23]The heart of this philosophical position is found in Aquinas, *On Being and Essence* (Toronto: The Pontifical Institute of Medieval Studies, 1949).

[24]Mortimer Adler, "In Defense of Philosophy of Education," in *Philosophies of Education*, part 1, ed. N. B. Henry (Chicago: National Society for the Study of Education, 1942), p. 211.

[25]William McGucken, "The Philosophy of Catholic Education," in *Philosophies of Education*, part 1, chap. 6.

[26]Jacques Maritain, *Creative Intuition in Art and Poetry*, Bollingen Series 35, no. 1 (New York: Pantheon Books, 1953), pp. 54-55.

[27]Ibid., p. 161.

[28]Jacques Maritain, *Education at the Crossroads* (New Haven, Conn.: Yale University Press, 1943), pp. 1-2.

[29]Jacques Maritain, *The Education of Man*, eds. D. Gallagher and I. Gallagher (Notre Dame: University of Notre Dame Press, 1962), pp. 111-12.

[30]See Maritain, *Education at the Crossroads*, pp. 10-12, 23, 29-38.

[31]Contemporary process philosophy offers a trenchant critique of the substantialistic metaphysics of Aristotle and Aquinas as yielding a static concept of deity. For a discussion of how this affects theology, see Ronald Nash, *The Concept of God: An Exploration of Contemporary Difficulties with the Attributes of God* (Grand Rapids, Mich.: Zondervan, 1983).

Chapter Three: Contemporary Philosophies of Education

[1]John Childs, *Education and the Philosophy of Experimentalism* (New York: Cen-

tury, 1931), pp. 50-51.

[2]John Dewey, *How We Think*, rev. ed. (Boston: D. C. Heath, 1933).

[3]John Dewey, *Art as Experience* (New York: Minton-Balch, 1934), p. 244.

[4]Van Cleve Morris and Young Pai, *Philosophy and the American School: An Introduction to the Philosophy of Education*, 2d ed. (Boston: Houghton Mifflin, 1976), p. 92.

[5]John Dewey, *Democracy and Education* (New York: Macmillan, 1916), p. 257.

[6]Morris and Pai, *Philosophy and the American School*, p. 280.

[7]William James, *Pragmatism* (New York: Longmans, Green, 1959), p. 201.

[8]Avrum Stroll and Richard Popkin, *Introduction to Philosophy*, 2d ed. (New York: Holt, Rinehart and Winston, 1972), p. 373.

[9]For a further discussion of the fundamentals of morality, see Alan Donagan, *The Theory of Morality* (Chicago: University of Chicago Press, 1977).

[10]For a further discussion of enjoyable and admirable beauty, see Mortimer Adler, *Six Great Ideas* (New York: Macmillan, 1981), chaps. 15 and 16.

[11]There is a piece of traditionalist humor which envisions a child approaching an experimentalist teacher as the school day begins, asking, "Mrs. Simpson, do we have to do what we want today?" The potential tyranny of wants and needs is all too clear in this scenario.

[12]Morris and Pai rehearse this experimentalist agenda in *Philosophy and the American School*, p. 283.

[13]Jean Paul Sartre, *Existentialism and Human Emotions*, trans. Bernard Frechtman (New York: Philosophical Library, 1957), excerpted in Beck, ed., *Perspectives in Philosophy*, p. 447.

[14]Ibid., pp. 501-3.

[15]George Kneller, *Existentialism and Education* (New York: Philosophical Library, 1959), p. 59.

[16]H. J. Blackham, *Six Existentialist Thinkers* (London: Routledge and Kegan Paul, 1952), pp. 155-56.

[17]For a discussion of an existentialist theory of art, see E. F. Kaelin, *An Existentialist Aesthetic: The Theories of Sartre and Merleau-Ponty* (Madison: University of Wisconsin Press, 1962).

[18]See Martin Buber, *I and Thou*, trans. W. Kaufmann (New York: Charles Scribner's Sons, 1970; and *Between Man and Man* (New York: Macmillan, 1968).

[19]Van Cleve Morris, *Existentialism in Education* (New York: Harper and Row, 1966), pp. 117-18.

[20]See Robert Ulich, *Crisis and Hope in American Education* (Boston: Beacon Press, 1951), chap. 3. Ulich points out that education of the emotions is crucial for eventual self-actualization.

[21]Kneller, *Existentialism and Education,* p. 133.

[22]Jean Paul Sartre, *The Psychology of Imagination,* trans. B. Frechtman (New York: Philosophical Library, 1948), especially pp. 273-82.

[23]See Robert Lloyd, *Images of Survival* (New York: Dodd, Mead, 1973). Lloyd portrays the inner dynamics of teaching and learning art from a rather existentialist point of view.

[24]Ludwig Wittgenstein, *Tractatus Logico-Philosophicus,* trans. Pears and McGuinness (London: Routledge and Kegan Paul, 1961), p. 49, proposition 4.112.

[25]For a presentation of the central concerns of logical positivism, see A. J. Ayer, ed., *Logical Positivism* (New York: Free Press, 1959).

[26]For a presentation of general analytic philosophy, see Morris Weitz, ed., *Twentieth-Century Philosophy: The Analytic Tradition* (New York: Free Press, 1966).

[27]R. S. Peters, *Ethics and Education* (London: George Allen and Unwin, 1966), p. 15.

[28]Ibid.

[29]Arnold Levison, "The Uses of Philosophy and the Problems of Educators," in Joe Park, ed., *Selected Readings in the Philosophy of Education,* 4th ed. (New York: Macmillan, 1974), p. 17.

[30]This example is found in Samuel Shermis, *Philosophic Foundations of Education* (New York: D. Van Nostrand, 1967), p. 266.

[31]William Frankena, *Philosophy of Education* (New York: Macmillan, 1965), pp. 7-9. Also see Frankena, "A Model for Analyzing a Philosophy of Education," in Park, ed., *Selected Readings in the Philosophy of Education,* pp. 139-44.

[32]William Frankena, "Toward a Philosophy of the Philosophy of Education," *Harvard Educational Review* 26, no. 2 (Spring 1956): 95.

[33]Frankena, *Philosophy of Education,* pp. 7-9.

[34]Frankena, "A Model for Analyzing a Philosophy of Education," p. 143.

[35]Frankena, *Philosophy of Education,* pp. 9-10.

[36]Frankena, "A Model for Analyzing a Philosophy of Education," p. 141.

[37]Jonas Soltis makes this point rather poetically in *An Introduction to the Analysis of Educational Concepts,* 2d ed. (Reading, Mass.: Addison-Wesley, 1978), p. 82.

[38]For a survey and evaluation of the linguistic analysis of religion, see Michael Peterson, "Theology and Linguistic Analysis in the Twentieth Century," *Wesleyan Theological Journal* 15, no. 1 (1980):19-33.

Chapter Four: Toward a Christian Perspective on Education

[1]Tertullian *On the Prescription against Heretics,* chap. 7.

[2]See E. G. Bewkes et al., *The Western Heritage of Faith and Reason,* 2d ed. (New

York: Harper and Row, 1963).

[3]Daniel O'Connor and Francis Oakley, eds., *Creation: The Impact of an Idea* (New York: Charles Scribner's Sons, 1969, p. 7.

[4]The biblical view of history and morality are not the only points at which the Judeo-Christian religion can be differentiated from its rivals. For example, against the backdrop of religions of the ancient world (for instance, Babylonian, Egyptian), Hebrew faith breaks out of the mythical and magical understanding of reality. Primitive religious belief, outside of Israel, is characterized by the loss of genuine transcendence and all that this loss entails: a closed, cyclical universe; identification of gods and persons with nature; coercion of the gods and cosmic powers through ritual and magic; absolutization of the political state; and so on.

[5]For further reading on these topics, see Holmes, *Contours of a World View.*

[6]Yandell Woodfin argues that "a Christological focus for ontology" is clearly implied in numerous New Testament passages, such as those asserting that Jesus Christ is "the image of the invisible God," the one "through whom all things were created," the one in whom "we live and move and have our being." See his *With All Your Mind* (Nashville: Abingdon, 1980), chap. 4. In the Incarnation—God's becoming human—we see what it means to manifest the life of God in our own creaturely existence.

[7]For further discussion of this point, see Keith Yandell, *Christianity and Philosophy* (Grand Rapids, Mich.: Eerdmans, 1984), p. 175.

[8]Some theists have tried to establish a foundation of moral value by opting for a version of divine command ethics, the theory that the basis of moral obligation is the will of God. However, a theory of divine command ethics encounters a number of severe difficulties (e.g., the problem of how sheer willing—whether human or divine—can itself be right-making).

[9]Yandell, *Christianity and Philosophy,* p. 266.

[10]Cited in Mortimer Adler, *Six Great Ideas* (New York: Macmillan, 1981), pp. 112-13.

[11]For further discussion, see Michael Peterson, *Evil and the Christian God* (Grand Rapids, Mich.: Baker, 1982).

[12]See Maritain, *Education at the Crossroads,* p. 24.

[13]See Holmes, *All Truth Is God's Truth* (Downers Grove, Ill.: InterVarsity Press, 1977).

[14]Jerome Bruner, *The Process of Education* (Cambridge, Mass.: Harvard University Press, 1960). Bruner is not a realist, believing that the structure of knowledge is based in the nature of things. Instead he believes that the structure which knowledge has is imposed on it by the human mind.

[15]Philip Phenix, *Education and the Common Good: A Moral Philosophy of the*

Curriculum (Westport, Conn.: Greenwood, 1977).

[16]Arthur Chickering, *Education and Identity* (San Francisco: Jossey-Bass, 1969).

[17]We might conclude that modern college students are products of a visual and sensual age in which little abstract thought is required, and therefore establish an educational objective of gradually helping them develop more abstract thinking.

[18]Mortimer J. Adler, *The Paideia Proposal* (New York: Macmillan, 1982), p. 22.

[19]See Donagan, *The Theory of Morality*.

Chapter Five: Issues in Educational Theory

[1]It would be interesting to explore what the modern equivalents of the classical liberal arts would be.

[2]Richard Burke, "Two Conceptions of Liberal Education," *Academe* (October 1980): 355.

[3]See H. I. Morrou, *A History of Education in Antiquity*, trans. G. Lamb (New York: Sheed and Ward, 1956); Robert Nisbet, *The Degradation of the Academic Dogma: The University in America 1945-1970* (New York: Basic Books, 1971); Christopher Dawson, *The Crisis of Western Education* (New York: Sheed and Ward, 1961).

[4]See Marvin Stone, "Good News on Campus," *U.S. News & World Report,* 8 October 1979, p. 88; David Boroff, "St. John's College: Four Years with the Great Books," *Saturday Review,* 23 March 1963, pp. 58-61, 75; Hilary Thimmesh, "Education Is about Civilization: Lose Sight of That and You Lose Sight of Humanity," *The Chronicle of Higher Education,* 20 July 1984, p. 64; Christine McPartland, "Computer Skills Won't Keep You Off the Streets," *Campus Voice,* August-September 1984, pp. 15-17.

[5]Arthur Holmes, *The Idea of a Christian College* (Grand Rapids, Mich.: Eerdmans, 1975), especially chap. 4. Also, for a discussion of various aspects of the Christian conception of the integration of truth, see Holmes, *All Truth Is God's Truth.*

[6]Robert Paul Wolff, *The Ideal of the University* (Boston: Beacon Press, 1969), pp. 76-79.

[7]For a fascinating proposal along these lines (called a trilinear curriculum), see Warren B. Martin, *College of Character* (San Francisco: Jossey-Bass, 1982), chap. 7.

[8]E. Harris Harbison, "Liberal Education and Christian Education," in *The Christian Idea of Education,* ed. Edmund Fuller (New Haven, Conn.: Yale University Press), p. 60.

[9]John Childs, *Education and Morals* (New York: John Wiley and Sons, 1967), p. 17.

[10]See Brian Hall, *Value Clarification as Learning Process: A Sourcebook of Learning Theory* (New York: Paulist Press, 1973).

[11]See Nicholas Wolterstorff, *Educating for Responsible Action* (Grand Rapids, Mich.: Eerdmans, 1980).

[12]Richard S. Peters, "Reason and Habit: The Paradox of Moral Education," in *Moral Education in a Changing Society,* ed. Niblet (London: Faber and Faber, 1963), pp. 46-65.

[13]Aristotle *Nichomachean Ethics* 2. 3-4.

[14]Philip Phenix, *Religious Concerns in Contemporary Education: A Study of Reciprocal Relations* (New York: Teachers College of Columbia University, 1959), pp. 60-61.

[15]Maritain, *Education at the Crossroads,* p. 39.

[16]Note that the Jewish attitude toward learning parallels that toward teaching. The book of Proverbs states: "Keep hold of instruction, do not let go; guard her, for she is your life" (4:13 RSV). The Talmud warns that "an ignorant man cannot be a pious man," indicating that spiritual suicide is the result of intellectual apathy and neglect (quoted from Morris Kertzer, *What Is a Jew?* (New York: Collier Books, 1960), p. 73. For further discussion of the Jewish attitude toward education, see Marvin Wilson, "The Jewish Concept of Learning: A Christian Appreciation," *Christian Scholar's Review* 5, no. 4 (1976): 350-63.

[17]Phenix, *Religious Concerns,* p. 80.

[18]B. P. Komisar, "Teaching: Act and Enterprise," in C. J. B. Macmillan and T. W. Nelson, eds., *Concepts of Teaching* (Chicago: Rand McNally, 1968), p. 77.

[19]For example, see James McClellan, *Philosophy of Education* (Englewood Cliffs, N.J.: Prentice-Hall, 1976). McClellan says that we can shorten the whole class of verbs denoting the intellectual acts which occur in teaching to a coined verb "to lect." This verb, taken from the syllable of primary accent in "intellectual," allows us to discuss the nature of the teaching concept. He discusses the teaching concept in terms of "lecting-claims" and examines the truth conditions for such claims.

[20]Abraham J. Heschel, "The Spirit of Jewish Education," *Jewish Education* 24, no. 2 (Fall 1953):19.

Chapter Six: Issues in Educational Practice

[1]See Edward L. R. Elson, "Life's Single Vocation," in *A Spectrum of Thought: Essays in Honor of Dennis F. Kinlaw,* ed. M. Peterson (Wilmore, Ky.: Francis Asbury, 1982), chap. 1.

[2]Maritain, *Education at the Crossroads.*

[3]Adler, *Paideia Proposal.*

⁴See R. Freeman Butts, *A Cultural History of Education: Reassessing Our Educational Traditions* (New York: McGraw-Hill, 1947), p. 624.

⁵For further reading on the separation of church and state, see Robert Cord, *Separation of Church and State: Historical Fact and Current Fiction* (New York: Lambeth Press, 1982).

⁶D. L. Munby, *The Idea of a Secular Society and Its Significance for Christians* (London: Oxford University Press, 1963).

⁷John Stuart Mill makes this point in *On Liberty*, chap. 2.

⁸For a common-sense discussion of relevant factors, see Barbara Thompson, "The Debate over Public Schools: The View from the Principal's Office," *Christianity Today*, 7 September 1984, pp. 19-23.

⁹See Hastings Rashdall, *The Universities of Europe in the Middle Ages*, 3 vols. (Oxford: Clarendon Press, 1936).

¹⁰For a fascinating discussion of the medieval origins of the concept of academic freedom, see Robert Nisbet, *The Degradation of the Academic Dogma*, part 2 (New York: Basic Books, 1971), p. 62.

¹¹Robert Hutchins is a representative spokesman on this point. In a notable address, he declared, "A university is a community of scholars. . . . Freedom of inquiry, freedom of discussion, and freedom of teaching—without these a university cannot exist. . . . The university exists only to find and to communicate the truth. If it cannot do that it is no longer a university." Quoted in David Fellman, "Free Teachers—The Priesthood of Democracy," in H. Ehlers and G. Lee, eds., *Crucial Issues in Education*, 3d ed. (New York: Holt, Rinehart and Winston, 1966), pp. 17-18.

¹²Nisbet, *Degradation*, p. 64.

¹³An interesting discussion regards the ways in which truth can need a helping hand. See William F. Buckley, *God and Man at Yale*, 2d ed. (South Bend, Ind.: Gateway Editions, 1977), chap. 4.

¹⁴See Philip Phenix, *Religious Concerns*, pp. 96-99; Holmes, *The Idea of a Christian College*, pp. 78-80.

¹⁵McClellan, *Philosophy of Education*, pp. 139-44.

¹⁶For further discussion of this distinction, see McClellan, *Philosophy of Education*, p. 139.

Chapter Seven: Christianity and the Pursuit of Excellence

¹W. K. Clifford, *Lectures and Essays* (1879), reprinted in B. Brody, ed., *Readings in the Philosophy of Religion* (Englewood Cliffs, N.J.: Prentice-Hall, 1974), pp. 241-42.

²John Stuart Mill, *On Liberty*, chap. 2.

³There is research to indicate that "threatening defense" is the best method

for helping students cope with objections tó their religious faith and world view—i.e., exposing students to criticisms of their faith and helping them work through them. See Wolterstorff, *Educating for Responsible Action*, pp. 60-62.

[4]Madeleine L'Engle, *A Wrinkle in Time* (New York: Dell, 1962), pp. 120-22.

[5]Michael Cain, "Psychic Surrender: America's Creeping Paralysis," *Humanist* 43 (July-August, 1983): 5-11.

[6]C. S. Lewis, *The Screwtape Letters* (New York: Macmillan, 1961), p. 8.

[7]Henri de Lubac, *The Drama of Atheist Humanism* (New York: New American Library, 1963).

[8]For a fuller account of the relation of Christianity and truth, see Michael Peterson, "The Lord of Truth," in *A Spectrum of Thought: Essays in Honor of Dennis F. Kinlaw*, ed. M. Peterson, pp. 47-64.

[9]Harry Blamires, *The Christian Mind: How Should a Christian Think?* (Ann Arbor, Mich.: Servant Books, 1963).

[10]See also Etienne Gilson, *A Gilson Reader: Selections from the Writings of Etienne Gilson*, ed. A. C. Pegis (New York: Doubleday, 1957), chap. 2. Gilson would say that persons who think Christianly have enlisted "intelligence in the service of Christ the King." Among the commonly cited traits of those who endeavor to think Christianly are a supernatural orientation toward temporal events, a commitment to truth and rationality, and a sensitivity to secularism.

Further Reading

General Philosophy of Education

Mortimer Adler. *The Paideia Proposal.* New York: Macmillan, 1982. Writing on behalf of the Paideia Group, which studies questions of educational philosophy, Adler points out the problems with contemporary education and advocates positive changes.

William Frankena. *Philosophy of Education.* New York: Macmillan, 1965. A brief but high-level anthology on issues relevant to education: human nature, the aims of education, freedom and discipline, morality.

James McClellan. *Philosophy of Education.* Englewood Cliffs, N.J.: Prentice-Hall, 1976. An application of philosophical analysis to the concepts of education, teaching, learning, moral education.

Joe Park, ed. *Selected Readings in the Philosophy of Education,* 4th ed. New York: Macmillan, 1974. A collection of readings by professional philosophers. The articles discuss the relation of philosophy to education, explore the structure of a philosophy of education, and analyze some significant problems in education.

Philosophical Perspectives and Education

Ernest Bayles. *Pragmatism in Education.* New York: Harper and Row, 1966. Considers issues such as the relativity of truth and value, education and culture, and the structure of educational programs.

Donald Butler. *Idealism in Education.* New York: Harper and Row, 1966. Reviews the history and essential teachings of idealism, considers an idealistic philosophy of education, and offers an evaluation.

John Magee. *Philosophical Analysis in Education.* New York: Harper and Row, 1971. Explains the aims and methods of philosophical analysis, shows its relation to education, offers analyses of key educational concepts.

Jacques Maritain. *Education at the Crossroads.* New Haven, Conn.: Yale University Press, 1943. In the Neo-Thomist tradition, Maritain argues for a philosophical-religious concept of human nature and traces its ramifications for educational theory.

William Oliver Martin. *Realism in Education.* New York: Harper and Row, 1969. Represents one strand of the realist tradition which is compatible with either naturalism or Neo-Thomism. Considers the nature of teaching and learning, the moral relations between teacher and learner, and the effectiveness of curriculum.

Van Cleve Morris. *Existentialism in Education.* New York: Harper and Row, 1966. Develops the existential philosophy of life, shows how it applies to educational theory, and considers its impact on pedagogy.

Liberal Education

Association of American Colleges. *Reflections on the Role of Liberal Education.* Washington: Educational Press Association of America, May 1964. A special issue of the periodical *Liberal Education* which includes significant essays by major educational thinkers.

Christopher Derrick. *Escape from Skepticism: Liberal Education as If Truth Mattered.* LaSalle, Ill.: Sherwood Sugden, 1977. A series of personal essays on the need for an assumed world view in education and the problems of skepticism in contemporary education. Espouses a Neo-Thomist brand of realism.

John Henry Newman. *The Idea of the University.* San Francisco: Rinehart Press, 1960. A reprint of a traditional classic by this Neo-Thomist thinker. Considers the ends of university learning, the branches of knowledge in interrelation, and the Christian dimension of learning.

Mark Van Doren. *Liberal Education.* Boston: Beacon Press, 1959. A competent traditionalist treatment of such subjects as the meaning of being educated, the shape of the curriculum, the art of learning how to learn, and the great tradition of liberal learning.

Robert Paul Wolff. *The Ideal of the University.* Boston: Beacon Press, 1969. Explores alternative models of university education, and explodes modern myths about value neutrality, relevance, university governance.

Christianity and Education

Harry Blamires. *The Christian Mind: How Should a Christian Think?* Ann Arbor,

Mich.: Servant Books, 1963. Argues for the need to think within a Christian frame of reference. Explores aspects of the educated Christian mind.

Edmund Fuller, ed. *The Christian Idea of Education*. New Haven, Conn.: Yale University Press, 1957. Papers and transcripts from a seminar at Kent School. Major thinkers discuss liberal education, personhood and community, faith and culture.

Arthur Holmes. *The Idea of a Christian College*. Grand Rapids, Mich.: Eerdmans, 1975. Discusses the Christian justification of education and applies the Christian world view to the issues of integration, academic freedom, vocation.

Education and Culture

Josef Pieper. *Leisure: the Basis of Culture*. Reprint ed. New York: New American Library, 1963. Discusses the immaturity and mindlessness of modern culture; recommends the cultivation of reflective intellect.

Richard Weaver. *Ideas Have Consequences*. Reprint ed. Chicago: University of Chicago Press, 1976. Discusses the way in which basic ideas and values impact every phase of life and culture. Condemns the shallow-mindedness of our age and recommends a return to traditional values and views.

Issues and Practical Matters

D. Beggs and R. McQuigg. *America's Schools and Churches: Partners in Conflict*. Bloomington: Indiana University Press, 1965. Instead of concentrating exclusively on specific, transitory issues, the authors raise enduring questions about the relation of church and state in education.

Jerome Bruner. *The Process of Education*. Cambridge, Mass.: Harvard University Press, 1977. A psychologist takes a structuralist view of knowledge and develops an intuitionist approach to the process of learning. The concept of the spiral curriculum emerges.

H. Ehlers and G. Lee, eds. *Crucial Issues in Education*. 3d ed. New York: Holt, Rinehart and Winston, 1966. Dozens of authors discuss all sides of current issues: freedom and control, religion and morality in public schools, gifted education, science and liberal education.

Warren Martin. *College of Character*. San Francisco: Jossey-Bass, 1982. Shows the need for institutions of higher learning to maintain their philosophical identity. Explores how philosophical commitments can shape the curriculum.

Philip Phenix. *Religious Concerns in Contemporary Education: A Study of Reciprocal Relations*. New York: Teachers College of Columbia University, 1959. Avoids superficial and conventional conceptions of religion and education.

Discusses parental, civic and professional involvement in the reciprocal relations of religion and education.

Moral Education

John Childs. *Education and Morals.* Reprint ed. New York: John Wiley and Sons, 1967. An experimentalist treatise on the need for deliberate initiation of students into patterns of moral democracy.

C. S. Lewis. *The Abolition of Man.* New York: Macmillan, 1965. This Christian thinker discusses how moral theory affects education and how education affects moral development in students.

Nicholas Wolterstorff. *Educating for Responsible Action.* Grand Rapids, Mich.: Eerdmans, 1980. A Christian assessment of current theory and practice in moral education. Develops a positive theory using the best research and insights available.